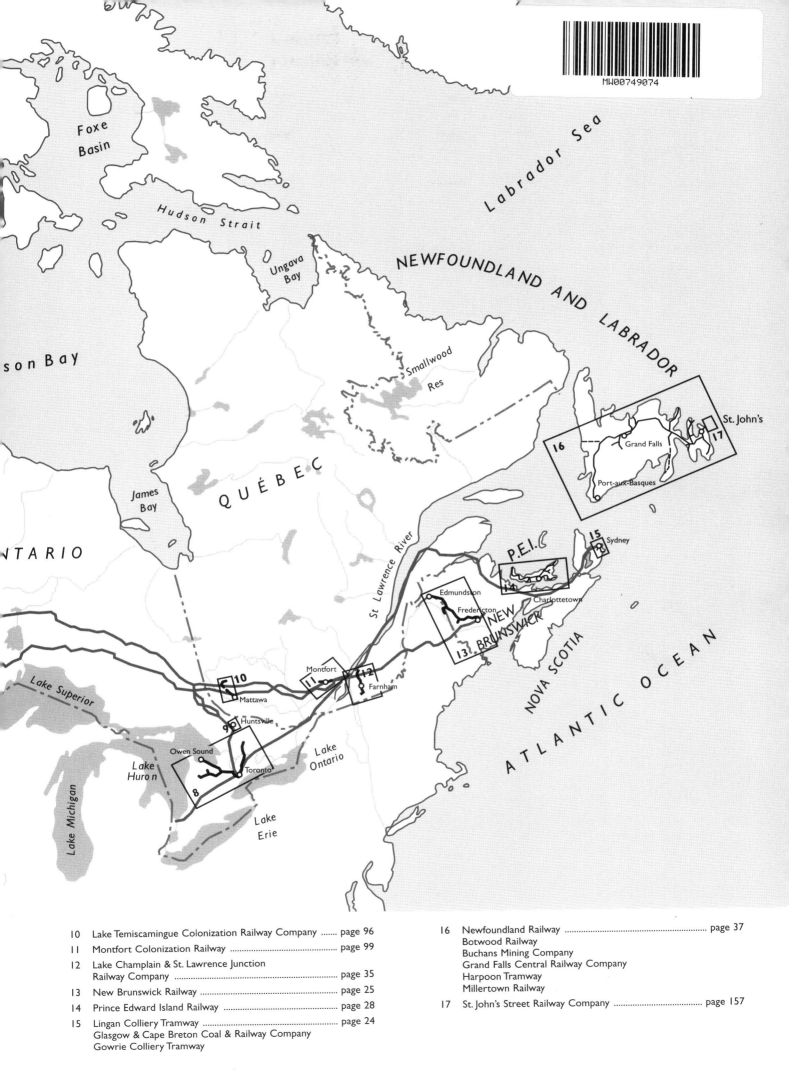

Narrow Gauge Railways
of Canada

By *Omer Lavallée*
edited and updated by *Ronald S. Ritchie*

A **Railfare** Book

Fitzhenry & Whiteside

Narrow Gauge Railways of Canada Copyright © 2005 by Fitzhenry & Whiteside

This book is a revised and expanded version of Omer Lavallée's Narrow Gauge Railways of Canada, originally published in 1972 by Railfare Enterprises Limited. This new edition was produced by Railfare for Fitzhenry & Whiteside Limited.

Published in Canada by Fitzhenry & Whiteside, 195 Allstate Parkway, Markham, Ontario L3R 4T8

Published in the United States by Fitzhenry & Whiteside, 121 Harvard Avenue, Suite 2, Allston, Massachusetts 02134

www.fitzhenry.ca   godwit@fitzhenry.ca

1   3   5   7   9   10   8   6   4   2

Library and Archives Canada Cataloguing in Publication

Lavallée, Omer, 1925-
    Narrow gauge railways of Canada / Omer Lavallée.
Includes index.
ISBN 1-55041-830-0
    1. Narrow gauge railroads—Canada. I. Title.
HE3704.L37 2005   385'.52'0971   C2003-903427-5

U.S. Publisher Cataloging-in-Publication Data
(Library of Congress Standards)

Lavallée, Omer.
    Narrow gauge railways of Canada / Omer Lavallée –2nd ed.
[160] p. : ill., photos., maps ; cm.
Originally published as Railfare, 1972.
Includes index.
Summary: Two dozen different railway systems are covered – listings of mileage, chronological and geographical facts about each system and locomotive information.
ISBN 1-55041-830-0
1. Railroads —Canada. 2. Narrow gauge railroads — Canada. I. Title.
385.52/0971 21   HE3704.L39 2003

Fitzhenry & Whiteside acknowledges with thanks the Canada Council for the Arts, the Government of Canada through the Book Publishing Industry Development Program (BPIDP), and the Ontario Arts Council for their support of our publishing program.

Printed in Hong Kong
Design by Ian Cranstone
Cover image by Christian Racica
Page 1 image credit: This painting by famed railway artist Wentworth Folkins illustrates Newfoundland Railway's Overland approaching Port-aux-Basques on the last lap of its 547-mile journey from Newfoundland's capital city, St. John's.

Contents

Legend to Locomotive Builders

American Locomotive Company (Alco)

Alco formed in 1901 with amalgamation of eight other builders: Brooks, Cooke, Dickson, Manchester, Pittsburgh, Rhode Island, Richmond, Schenectady. L&MCoM joined in 1908 as MLW. Knowing which Alco plant built the product is important.

Avonside Engine Company

Avon Street, Bristol. Founded 1837 as Henry Stothert & Co., 1841 became Stothert, Slaughter & Co. Loco building began, 1841 moved to Fishponds, Bristol, 1856 became Slaughter, Gruning & Co., 1866 became Avonside Engine Co., by when 600 locos had been built. Last works number was 2078, approximately 1,960 locos built by November 1934.

Baldwin Locomotive Works

Philadelphia, Pennsylvania (1831-1956) (an all-inclusive term for the several corporate names)

Beartown Mechanical Design

Durango, Colorado.

Black, Hawthorn & Company

Gateshead-on-Tyne. Took over works of R. Coulthard & Company in 1865, ceased trading 1896 (over 1,100 locos built).

Brooks Locomotive Works

Dunkirk, New York (1869-1901). Alco-Brooks continued production 1901-1928.

Canadian Engine & Machinery Company (CE&MCo)

Kingston, Ontario (1865-1878)

Canadian Locomotive Company (CLC)

Kingston, Ontario (1901-1965)

Canadian Pacific Railway Angus Shops (CP Angus)

Montreal (1904-1992). Named for R. Bruce Angus. Locomotive and equipment repair and building (last locomotive in 1944) (for detail see Lavallée, *Canadian Pacific Steam Locomotives* pp376-378).

The Climax Manufacturing Company

Corry, Pennsylvania (1884-1930)

Davenport Locomotive Works

Davenport, Iowa (1897-1956), licence transferred to CLC, Kingston, Ontario (1956-1968).

R. F. Fairlie

(1831-1885) exercised a patent between 1871-1889 in UK. James Mason (Machine Works) used patent in North America as Mason-Fairlie

Fox, Walker & Company

Atlas Engine Works, St. George, Bristol. First steam locos in 1864; 410 locos built by 1880, when taken over by Peckett & Sons.

General Electric Company (GE)

Schenectady, New York (1892-1920s); Erie, Pennsylvania in the 1920s to present.

General Motors Diesel Limited (GMDL)

London, Ontario (1951-1969). Still in production, currently as Electro-Motive London.

Grant Locomotive Works

Paterson, New Jersey (1863-1882); Chicago, Illinois (1883).

R. & W. Hawthorn Leslie & Company, Ltd. (Haw.-Les.)

Newcastle-upon-Tyne. Founded 1817 as R. & W. Hawthorn Ltd., became Hawthorn Leslie in 1820, 1884 became Hawthorn Leslie & Co Ltd. (2,611 locos built to 1938), 1937 purchased by Robert Stephenson & Co. and became Robert Stephenson & Hawthorn Ltd.

Hinkley Locomotive Works

Boston, Massachusetts (1841-1889)

Hunslet Engine Company

Leeds, England. Founded 1864. 2,236 locos built. Bought 2004 by LHGroup Services

Kaslo & Slocan Railway (K&S)

K&S shops (1892-1921)

Lima Machine Works

(1869-1891). Lima Locomotive and Machine Company (1891-1912), Lima Locomotive Corporation (1912-1916), Lima Locomotive Works (1916-1947), Lima-Hamilton Corporation (1947-1951), Baldwin-Lima-Hamilton Corporation (1951-). Lima (Lie-ma), Ohio. Established in 1869 as manufacturer of agricultural and sawmill machinery. Built first geared locomotive from Ephraim Shay's designs in 1878. First locomotive for a Class I railway built in 1917.

Locomotive & Machine Company of Montreal (MLW)

Montreal (1902-1908). Montreal Locomotive Works (MLW as part of Alco) (1908-1968), MLW-Worthington Ltd. (1968-1979), MLW-Bombardier Inc. (1979-1989). First diesel order 1948. Last steam order 1948, although boilers made up to 1955.

Mason Machine Works

Taunton, Massachusetts (1853-1890)

Montreal Locomotive Works (MLW)

See Locomotive & Machine Company of Montreal.

North British Locomotive Works (No. Brit.)

Glasgow, Scotland (1903-1962). An amalgamation of several builders namely: Neilson, Reid & Co. Ltd., Hyde Park Works; Dubs & Co., Queens Park Works; and Sharp Stewart & Co., Atlas Works. 2,000th loco by 1907, 3,000th by 1909, 5,000th in 1914, 11,318 locos by 1962 (plus 15,437 by the three constituent companies).

Plymouth Locomotive Works

Plymouth, Ohio (1914-

H. K. Porter Company

Pittsburgh, Pa (1866-1950)

Reid-Newfoundland Co. (RN Co.)

RNCo. St. John's & Whitbourne (1911-1916). Facilities also used by Newfoundland Railway.

Sentinel Waggon Works, Ltd.

(Sentinel-Cammell) Shrewsbury, UK. First patent steam unit 1906; by 1923 more than 7,000 built, mainly for road vehicles. 1923-1957, 850 steam locos built.

Vulcan Iron Works

Wilkes-Barre, Pennsylvania (1848-1954)

Vulcan Iron Works

San Francisco, California (1862-1870s)

Vulcan Foundry

Newton-le-Willows, UK. Founded 1830 as Charles Tayleur & Co., Vulcan Foundry, nr Warrington, 1847 became Vulcan Foundry; 1864 Vulcan Foundry Co., Ltd., 6,210 locos by March 1955. Now part of English Electric Co Ltd

George D. Whitcomb Company

Rochelle, Illinois (1906-1951), Eddystone, Pennsylvania (1952-1955) as BLW subsidiary

Westminster Iron Works (WIW)

New Westminster, British Columbia (1874-1943)

Editor's Note

ILLUSTRATION BY OMER LAVALLÉE

Payne Bluff, near Sandon, British Columbia, on the Kaslo & Slocan Railway.

WHEN ASKED TO UPDATE *Narrow Gauge Railways of Canada*, this Editor was somewhat taken aback. As a close friend of the Author, it was a given that Omer Lavallée had exhibited his characteristic thoroughness in researching material for the original edition. It was therefore expected that the work to be done would be to update the material, and so it turned out.

The suggestion has been made on occasion to add further railways (principally industrial lines) to this book. These suggestions have been carefully considered; however, it was decided to adhere to the parameters adopted by Omer in the original edition. Among these was that, for the purposes of the book, narrow gauge railways would be those having a width between the rail heads no more than three feet eight and one half inches, or "one foot narrower than standard gauge".

The reader should note that the Author's original January 1972 Foreword has not been altered and therefore the content may be found to be at variance with the updated references to the various railways.

In some cases the rosters have received major revisions. Every effort has been made to ensure accuracy and any errors or omissions are the responsibility of the Editor.

Finally, I would like to gratefully acknowledge the invaluable assistance of all those who provided information and/or photographs, without which this updated edition would not have been possible. Special mention must be made of Peter Byrne, Charles Cooper, the late Ray Corley, Allan Graham, Peter Hawksford, Steve Hunter, Michael Leduc, Don McQueen, Randy Noseworthy, Earl Roberts, Jim Sandilands, Bob Sandusky and David Woodhead. Special thanks to Eric Johnson, author of *The Sea-to-Sky Gold Rush Route*, for providing extensive information as well as many of his excellent colour photos, and to White Pass & Yukon Route for access to their colour photographs. Ian Cranstone's excellent graphic design skills made this new book sparkle. My thanks to all, and especially to my wife, Gilberte, to whom fell the task of producing the entire text in printable form.

Ronald S. Ritchie
December 2004

Foreword

THE WORDS "NARROW GAUGE", TO THE average North American rail amateur, bring to mind a mental picture of that type of railroading in what many view as its most sublimely classic form—as it was (and to a very limited degree, still is) practiced in the State of Colorado. The Denver and Rio Grande, the old "South Park", the Rio Grande Southern and others of their ilk have been the subject of so much bibliography and illustrated material that Colorado is widely considered to be the physical and spiritual home of the narrow gauge on this continent. Not undeservedly, I hasten to add, as a Colorado enthusiast myself and one of the dwindling number of the "select" who has purified his soul by having made the pilgrimage to Lizard Head Pass in a *"Galloping Goose"*.

Blind devotion, however unwitting, tends nevertheless to exclude other contenders. I had often considered advancing Canada's claims with a documentation of our narrow gauge systems, but procrastination is a familiar pitfall in a busy life. What was needed, obviously, was some single cataclysmic event to give priority to this particular project.

The provocation came about ten years ago when a Canadian, newly returned from his first visit to Colorado and hopelessly steeped in the lore of Marshall Pass and the Alpine Tunnel, wrote to me with a lament that went something to the effect that it was "too bad that Canada had never had any narrow gauge". That did it. My first reaction was a sense of disbelief and indignation. My second was to sit down and write a reply which became the story outline of *Narrow Gauge Railways of Canada*. Admittedly, its completion has taken a decade, but this manuscript is a product of pure research into primary sources—builders' lists, government reports, *Poor's Manuals*, interviews with employees and veterans, and on-the-spot investigation from Newfoundland to the Yukon and Alaska.

This story is intended to support the claim that Canada, and specifically the Province of Ontario, was the birthplace of the first narrow gauge steam-operated public railway in North America (July 1871). Additionally, it advances the argument that the introduction of a steam locomotive to the Lingan Colliery Tramway in Cape Breton in 1866 may well allow Canada to claim the first narrow gauge steam-operated

railway in the Western Hemisphere. Moreover, our country still possesses North America's largest network of narrow gauge lines in its three remaining common carrier systems. These modernized systems show every promise of remaining in use for years to come; over them, I am happy to relate, the spectre of abandonment has yet to appear.

This account may best be described as a "survey course" about Canadian narrow gauges; therefore, it does not claim to be complete in every particular. Those systems are included whose operations were reported annually in statistical summaries published by the federal government. Moreover, the work is a descriptive physical history and makes no pretense at economic or financial analysis. Outside its scope are private railways in purely industrial applications such as logging, plants, mines and quarries.

The purpose of this treatise is to interest and inform those unacquainted with its subject, but it would be gratifying if an ancillary effect would be to stimulate interest among its readers to investigate individual lines in greater detail with the aim of producing more detailed works.

I apologize to my friends in the United States for seemingly "upstaging" the Denver & Rio Grande in my references to the pioneer role of Canadian lines. In truth, the railways of Colorado have few more ardent admirers than me, my introduction dating back two decades, when I visited the small and isolated D&RG network centered on Montrose, Colorado. And though it was of no avail, I count myself among those from "north of the border" who, at the request of friends in the United States, wrote letters to senators and congressmen in a futile attempt to have the Rio Grande Southern retained as a tourist attraction.

Since the subject of one of my first railway photos is a Bridgton & Harrison two-foot gauge Reo railcar at Bridgton Junction, Maine, in the summer of 1939, I have sustained an interest in the two-foot carriers in that State, nourished by liberal doses of the writings of the legendary Linwood W. Moody.

Among the railways still happily in existence, I must mention the East Broad Top Railway at Rockhill Furnace, Pennsylvania, not only because its rails are of the three-foot configuration but because, as far as I am concerned at least, it has no peer on this continent among "preserved" railways for credibility and

To the memory of my father, who showed me my first narrow gauge train in July 1939, and thus introduced me to a facet of my hobby that has always provided a particular fascination.

Diesels haul Train 101 "The Caribou" westward-bound at Gaff Topsail, Newfoundland in June 1967.

authenticity in the visual appearance of its locomotives, cars and property, and in the deportment of its personnel. One of the few places remaining where one can savour the real atmosphere of the narrow gauge as our North American ancestors knew it is by riding in the observation room of the *"Orbisonia"*, the EBT's impeccable, Billmeyer & Small-built official car as its train "roller-skates" through an autumnal mountainous Pennsylvania countryside with the rails all but hidden in fallen leaves of every hue.

My attachment to small width systems extends to other continents as well and includes personal acquaintances with the Ffestiniog, Talyllyn and other preserved railway by-ways in the United Kingdom, as well as the steam and electric lines which perform such prodigious feats of hill-climbing in the Alps.

I must express my thanks to my associates for their assistance. To Ray Corley for reading the manuscript, correcting the rosters and generally carrying out his characteristic minute analysis of everything. To Dave Henderson for his unique artistic and layout competence, to which he gives such devotion. For the lines in the Maritimes, I have drawn extensively from field notes researched originally by a former friend, colleague and conspicuous historian in his own right, the late Robert R. Brown.

In the field of graphics, Tony Clegg did the profiles and the map of Canada, Jim Brown processed many of the photographs and shared his skills as a picture editor, while Bob Sandusky's meticulous drawings ornament the text where there is a paucity of illustrative material.

The suppliers of material include, among many others, Major C. Warren Anderson of Sussex, New Brunswick; W. H. Converse of Seattle, Washington; Cornelius Hauck of the Colorado Railroad Museum; J. Norman Lowe of Canadian National Railways; and Carl Mulvihill of Skagway, Alaska. Kenneth Heard helped with research.

As is usual in works of this kind, other assistance was forthcoming from many interested individuals and I acknowledge my debt to all, named or unnamed.

January 1972

A steamer passenger's first introduction to the White Pass & Yukon Route was the view of the train from the ship as it stood on the wharf at Skagway, Alaska. The locomotive fusses impatiently—seemingly eager to be off and about the serious business of climbing to the summit of White Pass, portal of the legendary Klondike.

"Narrow Gauge"...

The Narrow Gauge in a Global Context

The science of railways, as one of the prime by-products of the Industrial Revolution, has achieved an enviable degree of standardization, one which is attainable only by a technical form which has been in practical use for a century and a half. The layman marvels (if indeed he is even aware of it) at the fact that rolling stock of a hundred different systems can come together in a railway yard and be assembled into a train that can go anywhere on any of the represented systems. This is particularly true in North America where standards-making associations, beginning more than a century ago, determined that motive power and rolling stock would conform to fixed extremes of height and width and have common couplers and coupler heights as well as compatible brake systems. Corresponding minimum clearances were set up for structures; accounting procedures for interline book-keeping and operating rules based on a standard code were all necessary concomitants.

One of the chief features of community of practice on this continent is in the gauge of the track—the width between the rails. All but a negligible amount of mileage now in use in North America is built to the so-called Standard Gauge, which was made popular by the renowned Stephensons in England a century and a half ago, and represents the width of 4'8½", or 1.435 metres, between the rail heads.

On other continents, there is more diversity and Standard Gauge exists beside other widths, both wider and narrower. Without touching on gauges used in mines, on industrial systems, or on miniature railways, railway gauges may be said to range from 1'11½" (60 centimetres) still to be seen in many parts of the world, to the now-extinct 7'0¼" gauge devised by Isambard Kingdom Brunel, the greatest of the broad gauge protagonists, for the Great Western Railway in England. There were some isolated examples of gauges even wider than this. Notable contemporary divergences from Standard Gauge on the wide side include the railways of India, Brazil, Argentina, Chile, Spain, Portugal, Australia, Finland and Russia. The Russians are often blamed for obstinacy in the retention of their 5'0" width of track, but it was in fact an American, Major Whistler (father of the artist who immortalized himself by painting a picture of his mother), who introduced it in that nation in the Tsarist period. The continent of Africa is mostly narrow gauge, much of it on the 3'6" width. Next in popularity is the 1-metre gauge (39⅜") which can be found to a greater or lesser extent on every continent except North America. These other usages notwithstanding, the Stephenson width of 56½" is still entitled to be called Standard Gauge because it is now used on an estimated six out of every ten miles of the world's railways.

In the history of narrow gauges, it is usual to give priority to the Ffestiniog "Toy" railway in North Wales. This line, opened as an animal and gravity-powered tramroad in 1836 to bring slate from the quarries of Blaenau Ffestiniog down to Cardigan Bay at Portmadoc, was of two-foot gauge; today, it is 60 cm, or one-half inch narrower. In 1863, it introduced steam locomotives to the operation; these engines, happily preserved today, are generally accepted as the first true[1] narrow gauge locomotives to be operated in regular service other than experimentally. This latter distinction is important because it is not generally known that among Trevithick's pioneer tramway locomotives in England, an engine operated on the lines of the works at Coalbrookdale in 1802 had a track gauge of 3'1".

While opinions differed as to the utility of the broad gauge railway, the advantages of narrow gauge systems were more apparent. Particularly compelling was the argument of economy of operation, because of the lightness of the rolling stock and track, and the easy adaptability of right-of-way to the general contour of the land, without expensive engineering. In the author's mind, there are few more striking examples of the latter feature than the Newfoundland lines of Canadian National.

Too, the narrow gauge held out the promise of upgrading to standard width after the railway had become established and its traffic volume increased. This evolution was in fact characteristic of most of Canada's narrow gauge lines; comparatively few were abandoned as narrow gauges.

NOTES:

1. Arbitrarily, at least a foot narrower than standard. The Delaware & Hudson, for instance, used a gauge of 4'3" in northeastern Pennsylvania.

Narrow Gauge in Canada

When the first public railway in Canada was opened to traffic in July 1836, it functioned on a track whose gauge was the Stephenson one of 4'8½". The fact that the great majority of Canada's railway miles are laid at present to the same width would tend to suggest continuity. The opposite, however, is true; an interesting lack of uniformity has prevailed in the intervening period.

In fact, in the evolution of Canada's railways, there have been departures in both directions from Standard Gauge. First came the broad gauge, uniformly of 5'6", which was officially adopted by ill-conceived legislation passed on July 31st 1851, and which had the effect of coercing the construction of the Canadian trunk line system in the 1850s and 1860s to this arbitrary width. The chief advantage of its adoption, in the eyes of the legislators, was that it differed from the gauge of connecting American railways and so rendered Yankee domination of Canada, either in an economic or a military sense, impossible. We must bear in mind, of course, that in 1850 Canadians of middle age could still vividly recall the War of 1812; the vision of Uncle Sam in the role of an aggressor therefore had real rather than fancied implications.

The story of the broad gauge is another story; suffice it to say, that its downfall came in the early 1870s after laws had been amended, but not in time to save the private railway systems of Canada from the expense of converting tracks, locomotives and cars to the 4'8½" gauge. Desired free interchange of rolling stock with United States systems was now possible, but the capital expenditures involved were so onerous that some of the lines never really recovered financially, and were absorbed into other systems.

Faced with the sight of broad gauge systems struggling to return to Canadian gauge conformity at great expense, it is difficult to understand how advocates of another departure in gauge, this time on the narrow dimension, would meet with any success. Yet they did; moreover, the rise in popularity of the narrow gauge coincides almost exactly with the decline of the broad gauge in Canada. The significant year was 1866 in which, coincidentally, two otherwise-unrelated events occurred. One was the laying of a third rail to standard gauge along the main line of the broad gauge Great Western Railway through the southern peninsula of Ontario, enabling its trains to convey standard gauge United States cars from the Detroit to the Niagara frontiers. This marked the first physical step in the discard of the Canadian broad gauge network.

The other event was equally prophetic; as the third rail was being pressed into service, a one-mile-long Cape Breton colliery railway became the first narrow gauge steam locomotive operated railway in Canada, ushering in the Lilliputian railway era certainly in this country, and quite possibly in all of the Western Hemisphere.

In 1868, two years after the Lingan Colliery's 3'6" gauge locomotive was placed in service, the Baldwin Locomotive Works built a locomotive of the same gauge for the Averill Coal & Oil Company in West Virginia, and stated that it was the first narrow-gauge engine to be built in the practice of the works. This locomotive was followed by three more 3'6" gauge locomotives in 1869, built for the União Valenciana Railway in the Brazilian Empire. Thus, it would appear that Canada led its contemporaries in priority of application of narrow gauge steam locomotives as well as of small width public railways.

The two gauges commonly used in Canada were the 3'6" and the 3'0". While only six inches separated these gauges, their individual characteristics were far more divergent. For one thing, the 42" gauge was a British innovation and as its use spread around the world, particularly where English capital was involved, it became known as "British metric". Working practice tended to follow "old country" lines, as did motive power and, to a lesser extent, rolling stock design.

The three-foot gauge was more properly the narrow gauge of the United States, the prototype application in the USA being that of the Denver & Rio Grande Railway, opened in 1871. The D&RG's feats of mountain-climbing became renowned and as a result, Canada's narrow gauge lines in the West and in hilly terrain were patterned after the D&RG and its gauge. The inimitable cartoons of Carl Fallberg could as easily portray the Kaslo & Slocan or the Trail Creek Tramway. On the other side of the coin, operations on the Cape Breton lines and the Prince Edward Island Railway in its first years, might have been the prototype for the charming caricatures of Rowland Emett. There must always be the exception that proves the rule and this, in fact, was the Glasgow & Cape Breton Railway in Nova Scotia, opened in May 1871, which was a British-prototype three-foot gauge line, complete with Avonside plate-frame engines and centre buffer-couplings on its cars.

Nonetheless, mention of the three-foot gauge still conjures up visions of a Consolidation heading a passenger train along the Black Canyon of the Gunnison, or gunfights between railroaders and badmen. Three-foot has undeniable historical connotations.

Not so three-foot-six. Here we think of the Japanese National Railways' crack limited express *Tsubame*; not-so-miniature 4-8-2s working heavy trains along the New Zealand Government Railways,

"... clung stubbornly to mountain ledges ..."

"... washed by the salt spray of the ocean ..."

"NARROW GAUGE" ...

Keys to Inset Maps

or Beyer-Garratts up to tonnage capacity in the rain forests of East Africa.

Motive Power and Rolling Stock

As the world-prototype for narrow gauge, the Ffestiniog Railway introduced an interesting byproduct in the form of the double-ended articulated steam locomotive which was invented by Robert Fairlie. Two examples of this type, the only ones remaining in the world, are still in service on the Ffestiniog which is today in the hands of a preservation society formed of devoted narrow gauge amateurs.

In fact, the Fairlie Patent double-ender came to be regarded somewhat as a status symbol among the early lines. All of the four larger North American narrow gauge systems opened in 1871 and 1872 possessed one or more of these pioneer articulateds. The Toronto & Nipissing had its 0-6-6-0 *"Shedden"*; the neighbouring Toronto, Grey & Bruce had its twin sister *"Caledon"*. The Glasgow & Cape Breton had three 0-4-4-0s, smaller than the others, but built to the 36" rather than the 42" gauge. Finally, the Denver & Rio Grande had the 0-4-4-0 36" gauge *"Mountaineer"* which is said to have been a gift of the Duke of Sutherland.

An offshoot of the Fairlie double-ender was the single-ended "bogie" engine, on which the second boiler was replaced with a conventional tender body. The locomotive was still articulated, with the driving wheels (and sometimes a leading truck as well) pivoted under the boiler, and the trailing truck under the tender end. Those built in North America were known popularly, if incorrectly, as "Mason Bogies". To be strictly correct, they were "Mason-Fairlie Bogies" as the well-known American builder William Mason of Taunton, Massachusetts, only possessed the rights to construct Fairlie engines in the United States; he did not design them. Apparently, a similar license was held by the works at Kingston, Ontario, which produced two 0-4-4 single-enders for the Prince Edward Island Railway in 1875. Presumably, these could be called "Kingston-Fairlie Bogies".

An examination of the rosters in this book will reveal quite a range of locomotive styles and types. If the Avonside 4-4-0Ts of the Prince Edward Island Railway look as if they would be more at home pulling the private train of some East Indian native potentate, few will deny that, at the other end of the scale, not many 2-8-2s have more singularly pleasing North American lines than the White Pass & Yukon Route's 70-series locomotives. In fact, just about every wheel arrangement up to the 4-6-2 and 2-8-2 is represented in the stockbooks of Canadian narrow gauges. The diesels, too, form an interesting collec-

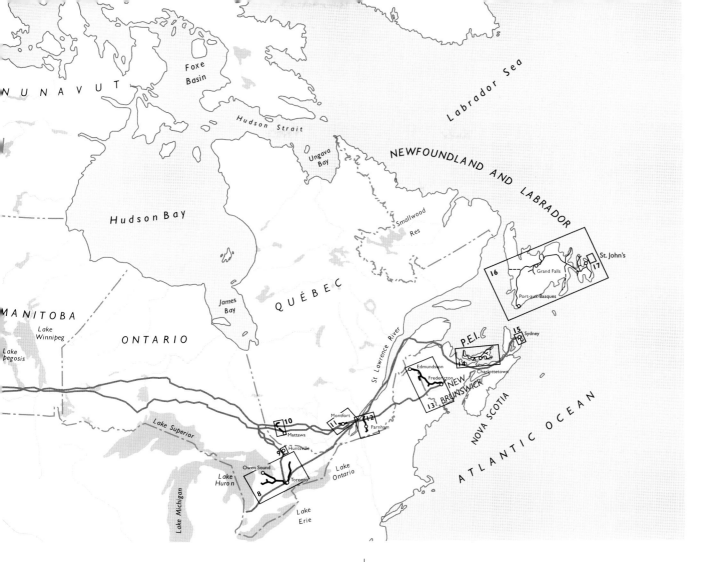

tion, from the noseless cab units of the WP&YR, to the adapted standard gauge bodies on Canadian National power used in Newfoundland.

Freight cars ranged from four-wheeled flat and box cars on the earliest systems, to container flats, refrigerator cars and depressed-centre cars. The White Pass & Yukon Route still clings to wooden, open-platform parlour cars of the 1890s, but the Newfoundland lines had progressed modernization to steel dining cars and sleeping cars with arch-roof contour (though no air-conditioning). In fact, about 1948, the Newfoundland's *"Overland Limited"*, freshly stocked with new rolling stock, could validly claim from a chronological standpoint to be North America's most modern train.

Postscript

Unlike the broad gauge, the narrow gauge in Canada suffered no simultaneous discard. As the time/mileage charts 1 and 2 will show, considerably less than half of the mileage disappeared over a remarkably wide range of time.

The "British metric" representatives, on the eastern seaboard of Canada, included the 700-mile network of the Newfoundland Area of Canadian National Railways, and the 22-mile long Grand Falls Central Railway. Another system is at the other end

of the country, running 110 miles through Alaska, British Columbia and Yukon Territory on 36" gauge rails. This is the White Pass & Yukon Route which, though dieselized and a pioneer of such modern freight-handling techniques as containers, still retains scenic and operating features characteristic of the classic narrow gauges of the Rockies in their golden age. From the point of view of nationality, the WP&YR is really neither "fish" nor "fowl", as it is a Canadian company operating a United States subsidiary which in turn owns all the motive power and rolling stock!

The status of the Newfoundland system as narrow gauge for a time appeared to be fairly secure. Canadian National had introduced facilities to interchange standard gauge and narrow gauge trucks under freight cars so that standard gauge cars could be used between mainland and island destinations without transshipping.

A troubling occurrence was the discontinuation of main line passenger service in 1969, and its replacement by a motor bus service on the more-or-less parallel Trans-Canada Highway. However, freight operations continued unabated until, in October 1988, Canadian National abandoned railway operations entirely. This action eliminated the remaining 704 miles of this system.

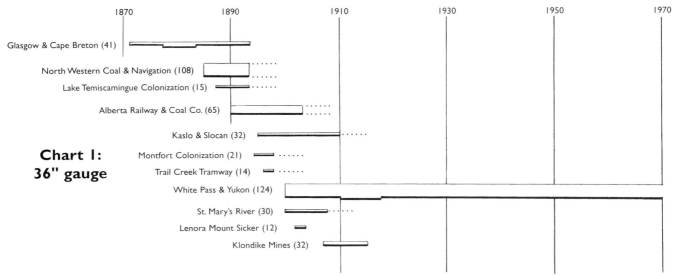

Chart 1: 36" gauge

Glasgow & Cape Breton (41)
North Western Coal & Navigation (108)
Lake Temiscamingue Colonization (15)
Alberta Railway & Coal Co. (65)
Kaslo & Slocan (32)
Montfort Colonization (21)
Trail Creek Tramway (14)
White Pass & Yukon (124)
St. Mary's River (30)
Lenora Mount Sicker (12)
Klondike Mines (32)

Time-Mileage Charts

Horizontally, the charts are divided into twenty year periods. Vertically, the individual railways are shown as blocks scaled proportionately by mileage, in each individual year. Figure shown in brackets after each system name is the maximum route mileage at greatest extent. Blocks extended by dotted lines indicate system converted to standard gauge. Where such lines are omitted, indicates system was abandoned.

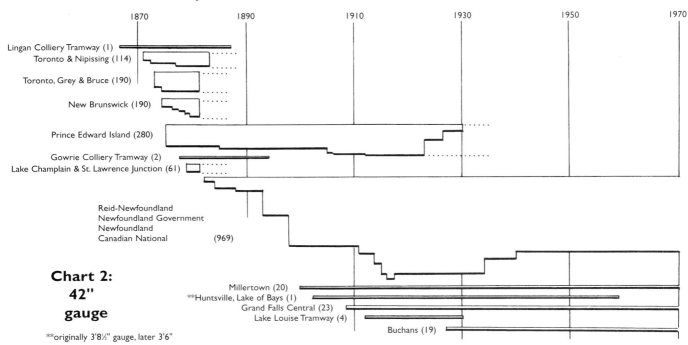

Chart 2: 42" gauge

Lingan Colliery Tramway (1)
Toronto & Nipissing (114)
Toronto, Grey & Bruce (190)
New Brunswick (190)
Prince Edward Island (280)
Gowrie Colliery Tramway (2)
Lake Champlain & St. Lawrence Junction (61)
Reid-Newfoundland
Newfoundland Government
Newfoundland
Canadian National (969)
Millertown (20)
**Huntsville, Lake of Bays (1)
Grand Falls Central (23)
Lake Louise Tramway (4)
Buchans (19)

**originally 3'8½" gauge, later 3'6"

The future of the White Pass & Yukon Route seems only slightly threatened by the probability that the Yukon and Alaska must ultimately be linked by rail with the rest of mainland North America. The implications of such an eventuality for the WP&YR are, for the moment, not at all clear. Thus it is agreeable to be able to say that the last chapter in the story of narrow-gauge railways in Canada has yet to be written. In fact, it may never be.

The following pages give an account, in chronological order, of two dozen systems whose lines clung stubbornly to mountain ledges, were washed by the salt spray of the ocean or ran across dead-flat prairie. Eight of our provinces had narrow gauge common carriers of one kind or another, Manitoba and Saskatchewan alone being bereft of this very distinctive brand of railroading. This section includes photographs, maps and memorabilia, as well as gradient profiles of the mountain lines.

Chronological and geographical facts about each system, with locomotive information, are provided for each owning company or authority.

A few selected dimensional drawings of narrow-gauge locomotives may give some encouragement to those miniature railroaders who select their prototypes from the ranks of the narrow gauge railways of Canada.

An appendix titled *Mining and Tourist Railways on Canada's West Coast* has been prepared by western Canada railway historian and author Eric Johnson.

•1•
Lingan Colliery Tramway

DRAWING BY R. J. SANDUSKY

Artist's conception of the appearance of the Black, Hawthorn 0-4-0T locomotive "Fairy".

WHILE THE TORONTO & NIPISSING RAILWAY opened its first section to the public in July 1871, a few months before the Denver & Rio Grande followed suit in the United States, and in spite of the T&NR's proud claim that it was the "first narrow gauge railway to operate on the continent of America", there had existed for some five years prior to this event, a narrow gauge steam operated colliery railway on the island of Cape Breton in Nova Scotia. This light railway, but one mile in length and built to the 3'6" gauge, was constructed in 1861 and extended from a mine of the General Mining Association to a wharf at the gap in the bar of Lingan Bay, northeast of Sydney.

The first five years of operation saw horses provide the motive power, but in 1866, the British firm of Black, Hawthorn built a tiny 0-4-0 saddle tank locomotive for the colliery, upon which the good Gaels of Cape Breton bestowed the name "Fairy".

This little locomotive pulled cars of coal from the mine to the ships until 1886 when mine and railway were abandoned. "Fairy" was then transferred to the Sydney Mines Railway, where it was standard gauged and worked for many years more.

Thus, well over a century ago and one year before the Canadian confederation became a reality, British North America fostered the birth of what may well be the first narrow gauge locomotive operated railway in the Western Hemisphere.

Lingan Colliery Tramway is shown on the map of Glace Bay, Nova Scotia area included with Glasgow & Cape Breton Railway Company account on Page 24.

Cape Breton, Nova Scotia's "black country", like that of England and Wales, was the cradle of Canada's railway system. Animal-powered tramways were introduced here in the late 1820s.

Lingan Colliery Railway

Lingan Mine to Lingan Bar, NS .... 1.0 miles   aban.

Gauge: 3 feet, 6 inches.

Chronology:

1855	—Mine at Lingan opened by General Mining Association.
1861	—Animal-powered tramway built from Lingan Mine to the gap in the bar of Lingan Bay. ("Lingan" is a local corruption of French "l'Indien").
1866	—Steam locomotive placed in service.
1886	—Mine and railway abandoned.

Steam Locomotives

No.	Builder	Year	C/N	Type	Cyls.	Dri.	From	To	Notes
"Fairy"	Black, Hawthorn	1866	3	0-4-0T	10x17"	36"	New	SMR 1886	A

Notes: SMR—Sydney Mines Railway.

A—When sold, locomotive was converted to 4'8½" gauge and was used until c1920 when scrapped. First locomotive on a permanent narrow-gauge railway in Canada.

•2•
Toronto & Nipissing
Railway Company

ORIGINAL: ROYAL ONTARIO MUSEUM

This painting by William Armstrong illustrates the celebration of the Toronto & Nipissing Railway opening at Uxbridge, Ontario, on October 7th 1871.

IN THE YEAR 1868, TWO APPLICATIONS were made to the Legislature of the Province of Ontario for the incorporation of narrow gauge railways. The first was that of the Toronto, Grey & Bruce Railway (q.v.), but the second was for the Toronto & Nipissing Railway, whose charter route contemplated a railway from Toronto to Lake Nipissing. Both of these legislative measures met active opposition by the members because of the narrowness of the proposed gauge, but ultimately the obvious benefits of railway into areas as yet unserved triumphed over purely academic considerations.

If the Toronto & Nipissing's charter had been second to be approved, it was also the second railway to get construction under way. Its first sod-turning ceremony took place at Cannington, Ontario on October 25th 1869, just three weeks after the comparable event on the nearby TG&B. To the Nipissing line, however, goes the distinction of being the first to open a section of line officially for public service, this taking place on July 12th 1871, when trains started

Toronto & Nipissing Railway is shown on the map of Toronto area included with Toronto, Grey & Bruce Railway account on Page 21.

Toronto & Nipissing's Fairlie double-ender "Shedden", No. 9, photographed in June 1879. Shortly afterward, this locomotive suffered a boiler explosion but was apparently repaired.

operating from Toronto to Uxbridge. The route used out of the T&N terminal in Toronto at Berkeley Street was that of the Grand Trunk Railway of Canada as far as Scarborough Junction, nine miles. A third rail for narrow gauge was laid in the broad (5'6") gauge track of the GTR main line. From Scarborough Junction, the Nipissing trains resumed their own rails onward to Uxbridge. The official opening ceremony was marked by the placing of triumphal arches over the railway at Uxbridge on September 14th 1871, although the event was not noted in the newspapers until October 7th. It was a day of public rejoicing such as has not been seen since the advent of the automobile, radio and television.

No time was lost in pressing onward with Lake Nipissing on the distant horizon. The close of the construction season of 1871 saw the miniature track at Woodville, near Lorneville, and the season of 1872 witnessed completion as far as Coboconk, 87 miles from Toronto. The service was officially extended to this point on November 26th 1872.

Plans were made to continue in the following year, but the panic of 1873 put an end to optimistic aspirations and Coboconk turned out to be the closest the railway ever attained to Lake Nipissing.

From an engineering standpoint, the railway was comparatively uninteresting, the country which it traversed south and east of Lake Simcoe being flat and largely agricultural in character. In 1877, using the charter of a subsidiary company, the Lake Simcoe

Junction Railway, a branch was built from Stouffville to Jackson's Point on the Lake.

In 1881, the T&N became a part of the Midland Railway of Canada, whose line crossed the Nipissing at Lorneville. The Midland immediately utilized the portion of the T&N between Lorneville and Scarborough Junction to earn a much desired entry into Toronto by laying a third rail along the Nipissing's track. However in 1883, the gauge on the Lorneville–Coboconk section and the Jackson's Point branch were widened to standard gauge, and the third rail for narrow gauge trains taken up on the Lorneville–Scarborough Junction–Toronto route.

The pride of the line was the double-ended Fairlie Patent locomotive *"Shedden"*, a behemoth by contemporary standards. It sustained a boiler explosion in 1874, killing three and injuring four.

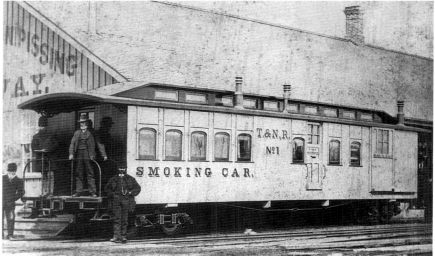

This image of Toronto & Nipissing car No. 1 is notable in several ways. It is a combination baggage / post office / smoking car and was built in 1872 by William Hamilton & Sons, Toronto, Ontario. This was the year that the railway commenced operation to Coboconk, 87 miles from Toronto. The building behind the car is obviously a part of the railway's facilities.

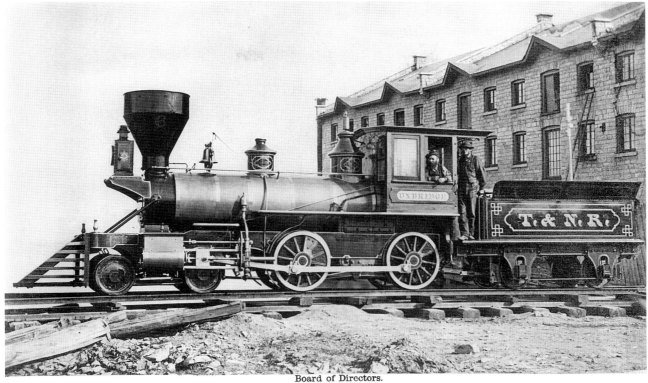

Board of Directors.

G. J. TANDY,
Superintendent

R. J. REEKIE, *President & Managing Director* ...... MONTREAL
HENRY YATES, *Vice-President* .... BRANTFORD

CHAS. GILBERT,
Secretary & Treasurer

OMER LAVALLÉE COLLECTION

Official portrait of Toronto & Nipissing's No. 6, "Uxbridge", taken at the Canadian Engine and Machinery Company's Kingston, Ontario works where it was built in 1871. Note that the light 3'6" gauge track on which No. 6 is placed, uses a broad gauge siding laid with inverted "U" rail as a "roadbed".

Toronto & Nipissing Railway Company

Scarborough Junction to Coboconk, Ont .... 78.09 miles @ part	Scarborough Junction to Toronto .... 9.00 " @
Stouffville to Jackson's Point, Ont. .... 26.91 " aban.	(3rd rail on Grand Trunk Ry.)

Gauge: 3 feet, 6 inches.

Chronology:

1868, Mar. 4	—Incorporation of Toronto & Nipissing Railway Co.
1869, Oct. 25	—Turning of first sod by Hon. John Sandfield Macdonald, Prime Minister of Ontario, at Cannington.
1871, July 12	—Line from Scarborough Junction to Uxbridge, 3rd rail on Grand Trunk and Toronto station facilities at Berkeley Street opened for traffic.
1871, Sep. 14	—Formal opening of line, special train from Toronto to Uxbridge.
1871, Nov./Dec.	—Line from Uxbridge to Woodville Junction opened to traffic.
1872, Nov. 26	—Line from Woodville Junction to Coboconk opened to traffic.
1877, Oct. 1	—Opening for traffic of Lake Simcoe Junction Railway Company from Stouffville to Jackson's Point and simultaneous leasing of LSJR to T&NR for 21 years from date of opening.
1881, Dec. 10	—Date of conclusion of consolidation agreement between the T&N, the Midland and other railways.
1881, Dec. 15	—Third rail had been laid between Scarborough Junction and Woodville Junction to allow operation on this date of first standard gauge train from Peterborough to Toronto via Millbrook and Woodville Junction.

Steam Locomotives

No.	Name	Builder	Year	C/N	Type	Cyls.	Dri.	From	To	Notes
1	Gooderham & Worts	Avonside	1870		?-4-?	10x18"	39"	New	?	+
2	M. C. Cameron	Canadian	"	83	4-4-0	11x18"	"	"	"	*
3	R. Walker & Son	"	"	84	"	"	"	"	"	+
4	R. Lewis & Son	"	"	85	"	"	"	"	"	*
5	Joseph Gould	"	1871	86	"	"	"	"	"	*
6	Uxbridge	"	"	87	"	"	"	"	"	+
7	Eldon	"	"	88	"	"	"	"	"	+
8	Toronto	Avonside	1872	$	4-6-0	14x20"	"	"	"	+
9	Shedden #	"	"	862/3	0-6-6-0	Fairlie	11½x18"	"	"	*
10	%	"	"					"	"	+
11	Bexley @	"	1873	938	4-6-0	14x20"	42"	"	"	+
12	Brock @	"	"	939	"	"	"	"	"	+

Notes:

+ —The Midland Railway Annual Report for 1883 mentions that two of these engines had been sold and that the remaining six were on hand for sale. These six presumably were disposed of after January 1st 1884.

* —These locomotives were damaged in the Uxbridge Roundhouse fire on January 14th 1883 and were subsequently sold for scrap.

$ —It is believed that Avonside C/N 932, 933, 934 were assigned to locomotives 8 and 10 and the replacement boiler for No. 9

—Named after John Shedden, first President of the T&N Rly, Co. who was killed in a railway accident at Cannington on May 16th 1873. This locomotive was a Fairlie Patent double-ended type, hence two boiler numbers. It suffered a boiler explosion at Stouffville on January 31st 1874, but was reboiled.

% —Details of No. 10 are unknown.

@ —Which locomotive is which is not certain.

1882, Apr. 1	—Effective date of consolidation agreed to on December 10th 1881.
1883-84	—Between July 1st 1883 and June 30th 1884, the line between Woodville Junction and Coboconk and the Lake Simcoe Junction Ry. were converted to standard gauge and the third rail between Woodville Junction and Scarborough Junction lifted.
1884, Jan. 1	—Lease of Midland Railway to Grand Trunk Railway of Canada.

•3•
Toronto, Grey & Bruce Railway Company

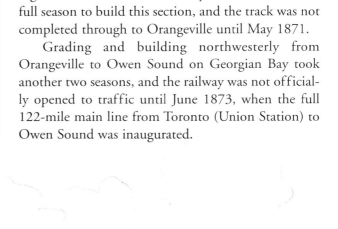

JOHN LOYE COLLECTION

Avonside double-ender "Caledon" pictured at Toronto waterfront shortly after delivery.

THE TORONTO, GREY & BRUCE RAILway, the slightly longer contemporary of the Toronto & Nipissing Railway, was inaugurated with a sod-turning ceremony featuring great pomp and ostentation on October 3rd 1869, at which his Highness, Prince Arthur of Connaught, officiated.

The route lay northward from Toronto to Bolton, turning westward into the Caledon Hills, then up the continuation of the Niagara escarpment to Orangeville. This escarpment was surmounted by the famed "Horseshoe Curve" near Caledon, a staple bend on a steep grade, which was the prime engineering feature of the Toronto, Grey & Bruce. It took a full season to build this section, and the track was not completed through to Orangeville until May 1871.

Grading and building northwesterly from Orangeville to Owen Sound on Georgian Bay took another two seasons, and the railway was not officially opened to traffic until June 1873, when the full 122-mile main line from Toronto (Union Station) to Owen Sound was inaugurated.

DRAWING BY R. J. SANDUSKY

The Toronto, Grey & Bruce Fairlie Patent "Caledon" is depicted ascending the famed Horseshoe Curve westward towards Orangeville, Ontario.

In May 1874, the 69-mile branch from Fraxa, near Orangeville, to Teeswater was completed, and the TG&B reached its greatest extent.

A series of adverse years convinced the directors that a change of gauge to standard width would be beneficial, and this was carried out on December 3rd 1881. The railway came under the control of the Grand Trunk Railway for a short period, but in 1883, it was leased to Canadian Pacific in perpetuity.

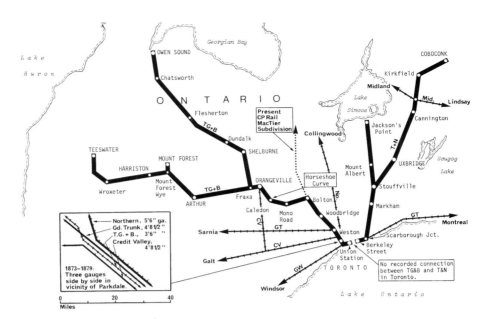

The section from Bolton to Melville Junction, just south of Orangeville, and including the "Horseshoe Curve", was abandoned in July 1932.

Like the Toronto & Nipissing, the TG&B had one Fairlie Patent double-ended locomotive, "Caledon", whose major visual difference from its sister locomotive "Shedden" was the inclusion of square sandboxes around the necks of the two smokestacks.

Many of the TG&B's narrow-gauge locomotives survived to be regauged to standard width. One of the accompanying photographs shows one of the converted Avonside 4-4-0s on a trestle on the North Shore of Lake Superior during construction of the Canadian Pacific transcontinental railway.

TORONTO, GREY & BRUCE RAILWAY CO. 4-6-0
Avonside Engine Co., 1872

Road Nos. 14
Gauge .... 42"
Type 4-6-0
Builder .... Avonside
Date 1872

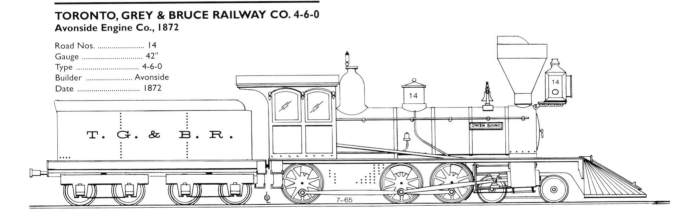

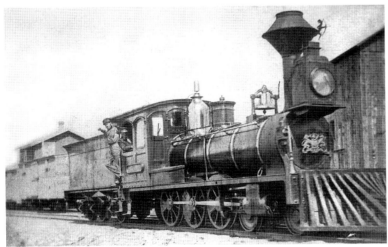

OMER LAVALLÉE COLLECTION

An unidentified Avonside 4-6-0 of the Toronto, Grey & Bruce Railway. The possibilities include engines 1, 11, 12 and 13.

Toronto, Grey & Bruce Engine No. 8 "Mono" was a 4-6-0 type built by Avonside in 1871. The very wide space between the second and third driving wheels was to accommodate the fire box. The locomotive was converted to standard gauge in 1882 and after the railway was leased to the Canadian Pacific Railway, it was renumbered to CPR's 1/159. In 1892 it was sold to the Parry Sound Colonization Railway.

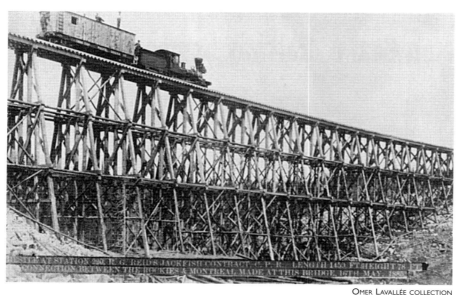

Toronto, Grey & Bruce Railway 4-4-0 No. 6, after conversion to standard gauge in 1881 and sold to Canadian Pacific (as No. 156) in 1884. Trestle is near Jackfish, Ontario, where CPR's main line from Montreal to Winnipeg was connected on May 16th 1885. This engine was sold in 1889 to the Pontiac & Renfrew Railway, a short line which extended from Wyman to Bristol Mines, in Quebec.

Toronto, Grey & Bruce Railway Company

Toronto to Owen Sound, Ont. .... 121.1 miles @ (part aban.)
Fraxa to Teeswater, Ont. .... 67.8 " @
Mount Forest Tank to Mount Forest, Ont. .... 1.2 " @

Gauge: 3 feet, 6 inches.

Chronology:

1869	—Incorporation of the Toronto, Grey & Bruce Railway Company.
1869, Oct. 3	—First sod turned by H.R.H. Prince Arthur.
1871, May 1	—Railway completed from Toronto to Orangeville.
1873, June	—Railway completed from Orangeville to Owen Sound.
1874, May	—Railway completed from Fraxa to Teeswater with Mount Forest branch.
1881, Dec. 3	—Gauge of railway changed from 3'6" to 4'8½".
1883, Nov. 1	—Transferred to Canadian Pacific Railway as part of the Ontario & Quebec Railway Company.
1932, July 22	—Section from Bolton to Melville Junction abandoned.

Steam Locomotives

No.	Name	Builder	Year	C/N	Type	Cyls.	Dri.	From	To	Notes
1	Gordon	Avonside	1869	799	4-6-0	11x18"	39"	x after 1883		
2	A. R. McMaster	"	"	800	4-4-0	"	"	"		D
3	Kincardine	"	1870	808	"	"	"	"		
4	R. Walker & Sons	"	"	809	"	"	"	"		
5	Albion	"	"	838	"	"	"	"		
6	Rice Lewis & Son	"	"	839	"	"	"	CP #156 1884		A
7	Caledon	"	1871	862/863*	0-4-4-0	11½x18"	"	x after 1883		
8	Mono	"	"	840	2-6-0	14x20"	"	CP #159 1884		A
9	Toronto	Baldwin	"	2534	"	11x16"	37"	P&ACRR 1881		B
10	Amaranth	"	"	2538	"	"	"	SLCo. 1881		C
11	Holland	Avonside	1872	935	4-6-0	11x18"	39"	CP #160 1884		A
12	Sydenham	"	"	936	"	"	"	" #161 "		A
13	Artemisia	"	"	937	"	"	"	" #162 "		A
14	Owen Sound	"	"	931	"	14x20"	"	" #163 "		A
15	Mount Forest	Baldwin	1874	3524	2-8-0	16x20"	41"	" #164 "		A
16	Orangeville	"	"	3525	"	"	"	" #165 "		A
17	Sarawak	"	"	3551	"	"	"	" #166 "		A
18	Melancthon	"	"	3552	"	"	"	" #167 "		A
19	Howick	"	"	3626	"	"	"	" #168 "		A
20	Culross	"	"	3640	"	"	"	" #169 "		A

Notes:
A —Locomotives changed to standard gauge 1881-2.
B —Sold to Philadelphia & Atlantic City RR.
C —Sold to Suffolk Lumber Company.
D —No. 2 "A. R. McMaster" on loan to Toronto & Nipissing Rly. for line construction September 28th 1870.
* —Fairlie Patent double-ended locomotive, hence two boiler numbers.

•4•
Glasgow & Cape Breton Coal & Railway Company

THUS FAR, THE THREE LINES referred to were all built to the 42-inch gauge, which was rather more popular in Canada than the 3-foot width that could be seen throughout the United States. Almost at the same moment as the Toronto, Grey & Bruce completed the railway to Orangeville, in May 1871, the Glasgow & Cape Breton Coal & Railway Company was completing its coal-carrying 36-inch gauge railway from the old pier at Sydney, Cape Breton, to its mine at Reserve, a distance of some ten miles. In the following year, a nine-mile branch was built from Reserve to the Acadia Mine at Schooner Pond, but this lasted only for one or two years. The G&CBC&R Co. had been incorporated in 1870 to work the mine at Reserve and to build a railway to Sydney and to Louisburg with branches to other mines.

PICTURESQUE CANADA

Mining scene in Nova Scotia.

Exercising the powers in its charter, the Glasgow & Cape Breton later extended its railway to Louisburg, reaching the old French Regime fortress town in 1877. In 1881, the properties of the

OMER LAVALLÉE COLLECTION

Train watching was a popular pastime in Sydney, Nova Scotia, in the 1870s, judging from this photograph showing one of the Avonside double-enders at a railway underpass. The photographer even managed to include his open-topped studio, just behind the locomotive.

G&CBC&R Co. were taken over by a new company, the Sydney & Louisburg Coal & Railway Company, but in 1883, the narrow-gauge line from Reserve to Louisburg was abandoned; in 1893, the Sydney-Reserve portion and the mines were acquired by the Dominion Coal Company and the railway abandoned completely. It should be noted here that this system had no corporate relationship to the later Sydney & Louisburg Railway Company, and the route followed to Louisburg was farther inland than the standard gauge line (see map). The Sydney-Reserve Junction roadbed was built upon in 1903 by the Sydney & Glace Bay Electric Railway, later Cape Breton Tramways Ltd.

As a 3-foot gauge railway, however, the Glasgow & Cape Breton was a little premature. No other railways of this gauge would be built in Canada until 1885, leaving the field clear for the 42-inch gauge systems, which were largely commenced before that date.

While all this activity was going on in Ontario and in Nova Scotia, the two Maritime provinces of New Brunswick and Prince Edward Island were undertaking small-gauge projects of their own. We shall take the New Brunswick system first, since its history is the simpler.

A good close-up view of a Fairlie Patent double-ender. This is Glasgow & Cape Breton Coal & Railway Company No. 3, built in 1872. The combination of articulated locomotives and light track evidently produced frequent derailments, hence the traversing jack carried as standard equipment on top of the right boiler, next to the dome. Locomotive was equipped with centre buffers and hook couplings.

Glasgow & Cape Breton Coal & Railway Company (1870-1874)
Cape Breton Company (1874-1881)
Sydney & Louisburg Coal & Railway Company (1881-1893)

Sydney Pier to Reserve Mine, NS	10.0 miles	aban.	
Reserve Junction to Schooner Pond, NS	9.0 "	"	
Reserve Junction to Louisburg, NS	22.0 "	"	

Gauge: 3 feet, 0 inches.

Chronology:

1870	—Incorporation of the Glasgow & Cape Breton Coal & Railway Company to work a mine at Reserve, NS and to build railways from the mine to piers at Sydney and at Louisburg, also branches to other mines.
1871, May	—Railway completed from Reserve Mine to Sydney Pier and opened for traffic.
1872	—Railway built from Reserve Junction to the Acadia Mine at Schooner Pond, but abandoned after one or two years.
1874	—Cape Breton Company formed to succeed G&CBC&RyCo.
1877	—Railway built from Reserve Junction to Louisburg.
1881, Apr. 13	—Incorporation of Sydney & Louisburg Coal & Railway Company to take

Steam Locomotives

No.	Builder	Year	C/N	Type	Cyls.	Dri.	From	To	Notes
1/1	Fox Walker	1871		0-4-0T	10x18"	43"	New	x 1890	
2/1	Canadian	1890	394	2-6-0	12x16"	37"	"	1898 re std. gauge and to DISCo. #155	A
2	Avonside	1871	907/908*	0-4-4-0	11x19"	39"	"	x 1894	
3	"	"	909/910*	"	"	"	"	"	
4	"	"	911/912*	"	"	"	"	"	

Notes: A—DISCo.—Dominion Iron & Steel Company
*—Fairlie Patent double-end locomotives, hence two boiler numbers.

over properties of the Cape Breton Company. It should be noted that this company was no relation to later Sydney & Louisburg Railway Co.

1883	—Railway from Reserve Junction to Louisburg abandoned.
1893	—Company acquired by Dominion Coal Company and entire railway abandoned.

•5•
New Brunswick Railway

ONE OF THE GREAT NATURAL ARTERIES OF the Maritimes is the Saint John River, which flows from its source in the Notre Dame Mountains of the Appalachian Range, to the Bay of Fundy, at Saint John. From the very earliest days of settlement in New Brunswick, a path, later a road, had existed over the Temiscouata portage from Rivière-du-Loup, on the Saint Lawrence, to the Saint John about ninety miles over the mountains, then down the valley of that river to the more settled areas around Woodstock, Fredericton and Saint John. The stage was set in this valley at an early date for a railway connection between New Brunswick and Canada, then separate colonies, but the dispute over the Maine–New Brunswick border, culminating in the Ashburton Treaty and its amendments, which gave over a large part of what is now northern Maine to the United States, forestalled any railway progress beyond Woodstock until the 1870s. It was in 1870 that the New Brunswick Railway Company was formed to build from Fredericton and Woodstock to Edmundston, evidently with the later intention of building over the Temiscouata portage to Rivière-du-Loup, which had been served by the Grand Trunk Railway since the summer of 1860.

The railway started at Gibson, on the opposite side of the Saint John River from Fredericton, and proceeded roughly north and west, cutting across the southward bend of the Saint John valley, in the direction of Woodstock; this town was reached in May 1873. Owing to the prior existence of service to the town by the New Brunswick & Canada Railway Company, the NBR was more popularly known to the public as the "Rivière-du-Loup Railway" in view of its obvious destination. Between 1875 and 1878, it was extended to Edmundston from Woodstock Junction, now known as Newburg. In 1876, it constructed a branch from Aroostook to Caribou, Maine, in conjunction with an American subsidiary, the Aroostook River Railroad, chartered

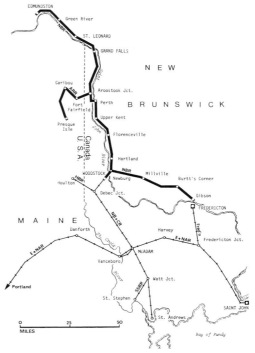

in 1873. The railway never reached Rivière-du-Loup; in 1881, as part of their scheme which would eventually result in a more far-flung New Brunswick Railway, the gauge was changed to 4'8½", and the little Fairlie-Mason bogie engines which had run up and down the valley were retired.

Saint John River, near Newburg Junction in New Brunswick.

New Brunswick Railway No. 7, an 0-4-4 Fairlie bogie, was the single-ended version of the famed double-ended locomotives. William Mason, of Taunton, Massachusetts, had the American patent rights to build Fairlie engines. No. 7 is shown at the works, loaded "piggyback" aboard a standard-gauge flatcar for movement from Taunton to New Brunswick.

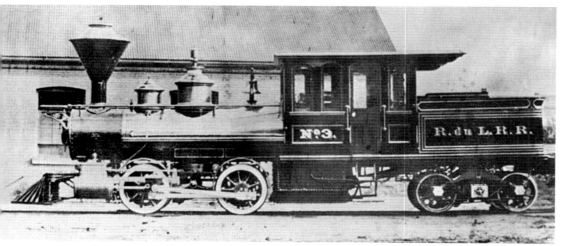

The first locomotives on the New Brunswick Railway were lettered "R. du L.R.R." for "Rivière-du-Loup Rail Road", a name which never enjoyed official sanction. No. 3 remained on the property for 14 years after the gauge was changed in 1881—long enough to be acquired by Canadian Pacific when that company leased the NBR in 1891. It was scrapped as CPR 531 but still narrow gauge, in 1895.

New Brunswick Railway Company

(Locally known as the "Rivière-du-Loup Railway").

Gibson (opposite Fredericton) to Edmundston, NB	166.7 miles	@CP *
Woodstock to Woodstock Jct. (now Newburg), NB	4.2 "	
Aroostook to International Boundary	0.7 "	

Aroostook River Railroad Company (incorporated in U.S.A. in 1874)

International Boundary to Caribou, Me. .... 18.8 miles

Gauge: 3 feet, 6 inches.

Chronology:

1870	—Incorporation of the New Brunswick Railway Company.
1873, May 1	—Railway completed and opened for service between Gibson and Woodstock, NB.
1875, June 9	—Opened from Woodstock Junction to Florenceville.
1876	—Opened from Florenceville to Aroostook, Aroostook to International Boundary and subsidiary Aroostook River Railroad in Maine from Boundary to Caribou, Me.
1877, Dec.	—Opened from Aroostook to Grand Falls, NB.
1878, Oct. 1	—Opened from Grand Falls to Edmundston, NB.
1881, spring	—Gauge of railway changed to 4'8½".
1891	—Lease of New Brunswick Railway Company to Canadian Pacific Railway Company.

Steam Locomotives

No.	Builder	Year	C/N	Type	Cyls.	Dri.	From	To	Notes
1	Mason								A
2	"	1873	489	0-4-4F	10x15"	33"	New	?	B
3	"	"	509	"	12x16"	36"	"	CP #531 1891	C
4	"	"	510	"	"	"	"	CP #532 "	C
5	"	"	526	"	"	"	"	CP #533 "	C
6	"	"	527	"	"	"	"	HN&P?	D
7	"	"	531	"	"	42"	"	?	B
8	"	"	532	"	"	"	"	?	B
9	Baldwin	12/1877	4211	2-6-0	14x18"	41"	"	lost at sea 1882	E
10	"	5/1878	4345	"	"	"	"	HGR #12 1881	E

Notes:
A—Identity of #1 unknown but believed to have been a Mason 0-4-4F, possibly acquired second hand.
B—Disposition unknown but two identical locomotives were sold in 1881 to PEI Ry. and hence are probably #7 and #8. Remaining locomotives may have gone to Newfoundland.
C—#3, #4 and #5 still on NBR property when line leased by Canadian Pacific. Allotted CP numbers 531, 532 and 533 and scrapped 1895, apparently before being relettered or regauged.
D—Believed sold c1882 to Herkimer, Newport & Poland Ry. (USA) as "Henry Dexter".
E—#9 sold Harbour Grace Ry. in 1882 but vessel lost in Gulf of Saint Lawrence. #10 also sold to Harbour Grace Ry. in 1881 and became its #12.
Locomotives #2-8 inclusive, probably also #1, were Mason-Fairlie Bogies.

<h1 style="text-align:center">•6•</h1>

Prince Edward Island Railway

THE LAST OF THE LARGE NARROW GAUGE railway projects to be undertaken in the 1870s was also destined to last the longest; this, the Prince Edward Island Railway, also enjoyed a political and financial career which was very checkered, largely arising out of the fact that the Island Province was not really able to support a railway of any kind then, or for a long time afterward.

From the point of view of extent, the narrow-gauge railway system of Prince Edward Island was second only to that of Newfoundland. Uniquely, the PEIR was also the only public railway ever to function in this Province, and as far as the author knows, the only railway of any kind, either public or private.

Prince Edward Island embarked on its railway system precipitately, in 1870, three years after it had declined to join the new Dominion of Canada. In the course of the spring, summer and autumn of this year, the Island Parliament chartered its own government railway, awarded contracts to willing takers, and turned the first sod of what was later to prove a rather

impulsive undertaking. The railway was subsidized by the mile, and the location left largely in the hands of the contractors, who quite naturally tried to squeeze every bit of railway they could into the area available. Work went ahead in 1871, 1872 and 1873 with a line being built from Tignish, at the western tip of the Island, to Souris, at its eastern end. It wound about from coast to coast in an almost aimless manner; where the Island was too wide even for such obvious winding, branches were built, as from Royalty Junction to the capital, Charlottetown, and from Mount Stewart to Georgetown.

By 1873, the situation had got quite out of hand —the projected railways were built, but were largely unequipped either with motive power or rolling stock, or facilities apart from the tracks themselves. A way out of the dilemma suggested itself, and thus Prince Edward Island applied for admission to the Dominion of Canada, including among the conditions that the Dominion government should at once take over the PEIR and operate it for the Islanders.

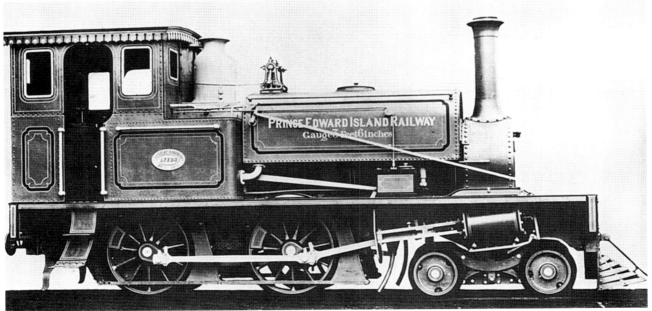

OMER LAVALLÉE COLLECTION

The first locomotives on the Prince Edward Island Railway were 4-4-0Ts built by the Hunslet Engine Company of Leeds, England in 1872, and would have looked more at home heading the private train of some Oriental potentate, than in mixed service in Canada's smallest province. At work, also, they proved to be more ornamental than useful and were retired, some finding their way to less exacting tasks in Newfoundland and Cape Breton.

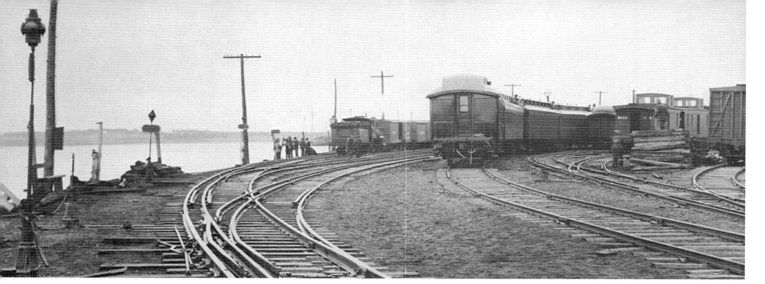

Charlottetown yard, with narrow gauge 4-4-0 switching, and coaches of standard gauge Charlottetown–Borden–mainland passenger train in centre.

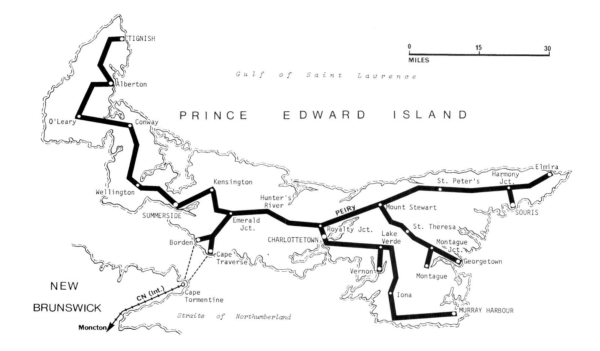

Double-gauge trackage in Summerside yard with a standard gauge 4-6-0, Canadian Government Railways No. 4522, approaching on the main line.

The east switch at Emerald Junction: line at left goes to Borden, that on right to Summerside. A narrow gauge work train headed by an unidentified 4-4-0 is on the Summerside track.

The third rail was added on the north and west side of existing narrow gauge track. Such a rule of thumb gave no difficulty except at wyes where this orientation could not be maintained without a transfer of the third rail from one side to the other. Here is how it was done near the south switch at Emerald Junction: the standard gauge rail shifts from west to north on the wye connection to Summerside.

These photographs were taken in 1919 when the Prince Edward Island Railway laid a third rail between Charlottetown and Borden and Emerald Junction and Summerside. They show the complicated trackwork necessitated by a purely interim measure.

Another close-up of a main line double-gauge switch, Charlottetown yard, with a 42"-gauge 4-6-0 in background.

Wayside station at Colville, showing double gauge mainline switch. Note the movable points in lieu of a frog on the left-hand narrow gauge rail where it crosses the standard gauge outer rail into the siding.

While union of Prince Edward Island with Canada did come about in 1873, the railway matter was continued in negotiation until December 1874, when the federal Department of Railways and Canals formally accepted the Prince Edward Island Railway as part of the Government Railways of the Dominion of Canada. Some of the arguments used by Prince Edward Island to bring this about struck at tender spots in Federal policy. One of the most telling was the comparison between the 3,000-mile railway which had been promised British Columbia as a condition of entry into Canada in 1871, and the few hundred miles of narrow gauge railway which Prince Edward Island asked to be relieved of as the price of its partnership in the Dominion.

JOHN LOVE COLLECTION

The caption to this interesting old photo tells us that the Reverend Father Burke is assisting to remove snow from the Prince Edward Island Railway plow No. 9. The occasion, otherwise, is not known.

As a result, on December 29th 1874, 196 miles of 42-inch gauge railway, as yet unopened to traffic, were transferred to the Ottawa government. The latter spared no effort to get the railway into active use, and this came about in the first half of 1875. With the exception of a twelve-mile branch line opened in 1885, the initial system of almost 200 miles was completely adequate to the needs of Prince Edward Island for more than thirty years.

The first engines ordered by the railway were constructed by the Hunslet Engine Company of Leeds, England. There were six of them—all light, very colonial-looking 4-4-0 tank engines. They performed all services, passenger, freight and switching. The railway soon turned to engines of Canadian manufacture, however, when the British machines proved to be too light, and consequently more prone to failures. A seventh 4-4-0T, built by the Hunslet Company for the PEIR, was not accepted by the latter; finally, in 1877, it was sold to the Gowrie Coal Mining Company on Cape Breton, of which more later. Some of the others were apparently sold to Newfoundland in the early 1880s, when the railways were under construction.

In 1905 and 1906, the Murray Harbour, Vernon and Montague branch lines were put into use, followed in 1912 by the Elmira Subdivision. In 1917, the branch to Cape Traverse, which had been opened in 1885, was diverted to the new ferry terminal which was named Borden after the Canadian Prime Minister.

The existence of a narrow gauge system on the Island, only slightly more than half-a-dozen miles off

CANADIAN ILLUSTRATED NEWS

Cross-section view of PEIR tank locomotive built by Hunslet. (See photo Page 27).

The eight-wheeled standard locomotive formed the backbone of the Island railway's roster. Note the monitor roof on the cab of No. 28.

the mainland, came under close scrutiny at this time, and as soon as the 1914-18 war was concluded, the Canadian National Railways, successors to the Government Railway system which administered the PEIR, undertook to place a third rail on lines connecting the ferry terminal at Borden with Charlottetown and Summerside, the two principal towns. This necessitated realigning the track so that the standard gauge was centred on the roadbed, and for this purpose, rails which had been rolled for Russia, but whose delivery had been deferred by the revolution in that country, were put to good use.

The dual-gauge arrangement remained until 1923, when the decision was made to proceed with standard gauging the whole Island. The narrow-gauge rail was lifted between Royalty Junction and Borden and Summerside, and the Summerside-Tignish line was changed over from 42-inch to standard gauge. All of the eastern end of the Island was similarly converted in 1926, but the Murray Harbour and Vernon branches remained for four years more. The late Mr. Robert R. Brown, railway historian and the Canadian National police constable at Charlottetown, were the only witnesses to the arrival of the last 42-inch gauge train ever to run in Prince Edward Island on a day late in August, 1930.

The last standard gauge train ran onto the car ferry at Borden on December 28th 1989.

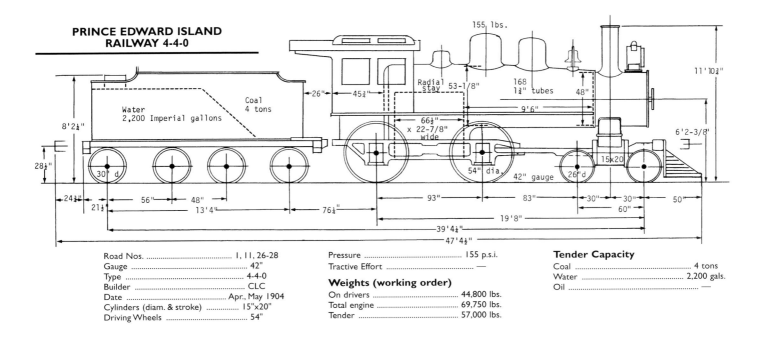

PRINCE EDWARD ISLAND RAILWAY 4-4-0

Road Nos.	1, 11, 26-28
Gauge	42"
Type	4-4-0
Builder	CLC
Date	Apr., May 1904
Cylinders (diam. & stroke)	15"x20"
Driving Wheels	54"

Pressure	155 p.s.i.
Tractive Effort	—

Weights (working order)

On drivers	44,800 lbs.
Total engine	69,750 lbs.
Tender	57,000 lbs.

Tender Capacity

Coal	4 tons
Water	2,200 gals.
Oil	—

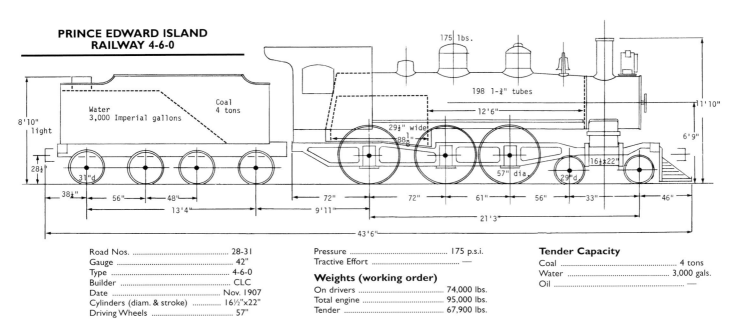

PRINCE EDWARD ISLAND RAILWAY 4-6-0

Road Nos.	28-31
Gauge	42"
Type	4-6-0
Builder	CLC
Date	Nov. 1907
Cylinders (diam. & stroke)	16½"x22"
Driving Wheels	57"

Pressure	175 p.s.i.
Tractive Effort	—

Weights (working order)

On drivers	74,000 lbs.
Total engine	95,000 lbs.
Tender	67,900 lbs.

Tender Capacity

Coal	4 tons
Water	3,000 gals.
Oil	—

CANADIAN LOCOMOTIVE COMPANY

Prince Edward Island's largest and most powerful narrow gauge locomotives were four ten-wheelers built by Canadian Locomotive Company in September 1918, of which No. 34 was one. As delivered, they were lettered for Canadian Government Railways, which was the designation used by the PEI lines after 1913.

Prince Edward Island Railway (1871-1913);
Canadian Government Railways (1913-1918);
Canadian National Railways (1918-1989)

Charlottetown to Tignish	115.17 miles	Charlottetown to Murray Harbour	47.66 miles
Alberton Junction to Alberton	1.69 "	Lake Verde to Vernon	4.43 "
Royalty Junction to Souris	55.03 "	Montague Junction to Montague	6.63 "
Mount Stewart Junction to Georgetown	24.07 "	Harmony Junction to Elmira	9.85 "
Emerald Junction to Cape Traverse	12.00 "	Diversion from Cape Traverse branch to Borden	3.27 "

Notes on Locomotive Roster

List is divided in two: (a) shows locomotives acquired prior to 1880. (b) shows acquisitions after 1880. This format has been adopted in the interest of keeping blocks of similar locomotives together. It will be seen that the PEI Ry. adopted the practice of filling gaps in its roster as a result of scrapping or disposal, with new locomotives, in order to keep locomotives in one consecutive numerical block beginning at "1". Road numbers in column (1) are those of PEI Ry./CG Rys.; those in column (2) are those of CN Rys. after 1918. CN Rys. classes are shown at the right hand side.

Gauge: 3 feet, 6 inches.

Chronology:

1871	—Government of Prince Edward Island authorized to construct Prince Edward Island Railway, to be operated by commission.
1873	—Prince Edward Island confederates with Canada and federal government agrees to take over railway as part of government lines.
1874, Dec. 29	—PEI Ry. officially transferred to Dominion government.
1875, Jan. 4	—Railway opened from Souris to Tignish, with branches to Charlottetown, Georgetown and Alberton Wharf.
1885, Jan. 22	—Cape Traverse branch opened.
1901, Dec. 31	—Alberton Wharf branch abandoned.
1905, Nov. 1	—Opened from Charlottetown to Murray Harbour, and branch from Lake Verde to Vernon.
1906, June 1	—Opened from Montague Junction to Montague.
1912, Nov. 25	—Opened from Harmony Junction to Elmira.
1917, Dec. 12	—Last 2.62 miles of Cape Traverse branch abandoned, and 3.27 mile diversion opened from Mile 9.38 to Borden.
1918	—Prince Edward Island Railway, as part of Canadian Government Railways, comprised in newly-formed Canadian National Railways.
1919, Sep. 18	—Third rail for standard gauge trains laid from Charlottetown to Summerside and from Emerald Junction to Borden.
1923, Aug. 11	—Summerside to Tignish changed to standard gauge. Emerald Junction to Borden and Royalty Junction to Summerside, narrow gauge third rail lifted.
1926, Aug. 22	—Royalty Junction to Souris; Mount Stewart Junction to Georgetown; and Montague Junction to Montague changed to standard gauge.
1926, Aug. 30	—Harmony Junction to Elmira changed to standard gauge.
1930, Sep. 27	—Engine #34 makes last narrow gauge run in Prince Edward Island, between Charlottetown and Murray Harbour, and branch from Lake Verde to Vernon. These lines changed to standard gauge completely eliminating all narrow gauge from Prince Edward Island.

Locomotives acquired before 1880

Nos.	Builder	Year	C/N	Type	Cyls.	Dri.	From	To	Notes
1/1	Hunslet	1872	84	4-4-0T	10x16"	42"	New	x prior 1880	
1/2	"	"	85	"	"	"	"	HGR? 1881	A
1/3	"	"	86	"	"	"	"	HGR? 1881	A
1/4	"	"	87	"	"	"	"	HGR? 1881	A
1/5	"	"	88	"	"	"	"	HGR? 1881	A
1/6	"	"	89	"	"	"	"	HGR? 1881	A
1/7	"	"	95	"	"	"	"		B
2/7	Haw.-Les.	"	225	"	12x19"	45"	New	x prior 1884	
1/8	"	"	226	"	"	"	"	x1885-89	
9	"	"	227	"	"	"	"	x after 1904	
1/10	"	"	228	"	"	"	"	x 1885-87	
1/11	Baldwin	1874	3535	4-4-0	12x18"	46"	"	x 1901-04	
12	"	"	3536	"	"	"	"	x after 1904	
13	"	"	3537	"	"	"	"	x after 1904	
14	"	"	3538	"	"	"	"	x after 1904	
15	Canadian	1876	159?	"	14x18"	48"	"	x after 1904	
16	"	"	160?	"	"	"	"	x after 1904	
17	"	"	161?	"	"	"	"	x after 1904	
18	"	"	162?	"	"	"	"	x after 1904	
1/19	"	1880	197?	0-4-4F	"	"	"	x 1899-1907	
1/20	"	"	198?	"	"	"	"	x prior 1899	

Locomotives acquired after 1880

Nos. (1)	(2)	Builder	Year	C/N	Type	Cyls.	Dri.	From	CN Class	To	Notes
2/1		Mason	1873		0-4-4F	12x16"	42"	NB Ry 7? 1880		x 1901-04	
2/2		"	"		"	"	"	NB Ry 8? "		x after 1904	
2/3	11	Canadian	1882	227	4-4-0	14x18"	48"	New	X-4-a	x 9/20	
2/4	12	"	"	228	"	"	"	"	"	x 9/20	
2/5	13	"	"	229	"	"	"	"	"	x 9/20	
2/6	14	"	"	230	"	"	"	"	"	x 9/20	
2/7	15	"	4/1884	294	4-4-0	15x18"	69"	"	X-4-a	x 2/21	
21	21	"	"	295	"	"	61"	"	"	x 2/21	
2/10	17	"	1887	326	"	17x24"	48"	"	"	x 7/23	C
2/8	16	"	7/1899	470	"	15x20"	"	"	"	x 2/23	
2/20	20	"	"	471	"	"	"	"	L-K 11/23		D
22	22	"	9/1900	496	"	"	"	"	"	x 2/23	
23	23	"	"	497	"	"	"	"	L-K 11/23		D
24	24	"	12/1901	520	"	"	54"	"	L-K 11/23		D
25	25	"	"	521	"	"	"	"	"	x 7/23	
3/ 1	10	"	4/1904	616	"	"	"	"	"	x 12/24	
2/11	18	"	"	617	"	"	"	"	"	x 12/24	
26	26	"	5/1904	618	"	"	"	"	"	x 12/24	
27	27	"	"	619	"	"	"	"	L-K 11/23		D
1/28 later} 2/19	19 }	"	4/1904	625	"	"	"	"	L-K 11/23		D,E
2/28	28	"	12/1907	781	4-6-0	16½x22"	57"	"	X-5-a	x 5/27	
29	29	"	"	782	"	"	"	"	"	x 5/27	
30	30	"	"	783	"	"	"	"	"	x 5/27	
31	31	"	"	784	"	"	"	"	"	x 5/27	
32	32	"	9/1918	1521	"	"	"	"	X-5-b	x 12/32	F
33	33	"	"	1522	"	"	"	"	"	x 12/32	F
34	34	"	"	1523	"	"	"	"	"	x 12/32	F
35	35	"	"	1524	"	"	"	"	"	x 12/32	F
36	1	Davenport	1910		0-4-0T	8x16"	24"	S/H 1918	X-1-a	HNP 4/30	G

Notes:

A—Some of these sold to "Harbour Grace Railway" 1881.

B—Locomotive refused by PEI Ry. and sold by builder direct to Gowrie Coal Mining Co. as #2 "Lassie o' Gowrie" in 1877.

C—CLC records say #10 re# 21 in 12/1898 but unable to reconcile with roster.

D—Five locomotives sold Lamoreaux-Kelly, contractors from Montreal, 11/1923. Reportedly used in construction of Bowater's pulp and paper mill at Corner Brook, Nfld.

E—This locomotive displayed at the St. Louis World's Fair, 1904. It was renumbered 2/19 in 1907 to make way for CLC C/N #781 given No. 28 in error. CLC records indicate erroneously that C/N 625 re# from 19 to 28.

F—Lettered "Canadian Government Railways" as delivered.

G—Acquired from D. A. Morrison, contractors, July 3rd 1918. Sold to H. N. Price, Moncton, NB.

•7•
Gowrie Colliery Tramway

Its British outline incongruous in a Canadian setting, "Lassie O'Gowrie" operated over a railway that was unsure of its gauge! (See text.)

ANOTHER CAPE BRETON SHORT LINE WAS the next narrow gauge railway to be opened to traffic. This line, only 1½ miles long and of 42-inch gauge, was built from the Balmoral Mine of the Gowrie Coal Mining Company, to Cow Bay. The mine and railway were both opened in 1877, and lasted until 1894 when the mine was purchased by the Dominion Coal Company, who abandoned both the mine and the railway shortly afterward. The two locomotives used were Hunslet 4-4-0Ts, similar to those first used on the Prince Edward Island Railway. One of them, put into use in 1877, was supposed to have been refused by the PEIR; the other, built in 1879, was apparently identical.

The Gowrie tramway is notable as the railway with the variable gauge—at least as far as the Dominion government annual statistical report on railways is concerned! For the fiscal years ending in 1876 and 1877, the gauge is given as 3'7½"; between 1878 and 1881 it is shown as 3'7"; and finally, in 1882, it became 3'6"! Variable axles?—hardly, but perhaps they literally measured the gauge each year and did it at different spots. The most logical explanation would be typographical errors in the statistics, but if so, the figures are repeated again in the summary of mileage of each gauge, after the detailed reference beside the company's name, in each of the years concerned.

Gowrie Colliery Tramway is shown on the map of Glace Bay area included with Glasgow & Cape Breton Coal & Railway Company account on Page 24.

Gowrie Colliery Tramway profile (Gowrie Coal Mining Company) appears on the facing page.

•8•
Lake Champlain & St. Lawrence Junction Railway Company

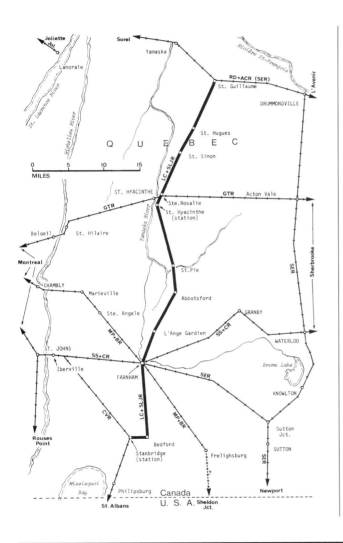

THE END OF THE FIRST DECADE IN THE history of narrow gauge railways in Canada saw the incorporation and building of the first such line in the Province of Quebec, extending from Stanbridge, on the Central Vermont Railway, a few miles north of the International boundary, northward into the fertile plain of the Richelieu River. This 42-inch gauge railway's economy was based almost completely on agricultural products, the principal traffic being hay intended for consumption by the thousands of horses used in the industrial cities of the eastern United States.

Extending northward from its CVRR connection, the Lake Champlain & Saint Lawrence Junction Railway first reached the railway hub of Farnham, Quebec, already served by the standard gauge lines of the Montreal, Portland & Boston Railway, the Stanstead, Shefford & Chambly Railway Company, and the South Eastern Railway Company. North of Farnham, at St. Rosalie Junction, the narrow gauge intersected the Grand Trunk Railway, and at its northern terminal, St. Guillaume d'Upton, Quebec, it connected with the Sorel-Drummondville section of the South Eastern Railway.

The narrow gauge line was opened throughout in October 1879, but its career was very short-lived.

LC&StLJ profile appears on the following page.

Gowrie Coal Mining Company

Gowrie Mine to Cow Bay, NS .... 1.5 miles   aban.

Gauge: 3 feet, 6 inches.
*Gauge given in 1876 and 1877 federal government railway statistical reports as 3'7½"; in 1878 to 1881, it is reported as 3'7"; from 1882 onward it is given as 3'6".

Chronology:

1864	—Gowrie Mine opened using cable tram.
1877	—Balmoral Shaft sunk about one mile from the shore of Cow Bay and railway built for locomotive operation.
1894, Mar. 1	—GCM Co. purchased by Dominion Coal Company who closed mine shortly afterward and abandoned railway.

Steam Locomotives

No.	Builder	Year	C/N	Type	Cyls.	Dri.	From	To	Notes
1	Hunslet	1872	95	4-4-0T	10x16"	42"	x 1894		A
2	"	1879	228	"	"	"	"		B

Notes: A—Named "*Lassie o' Gowrie*"; said to have been ordered by the Prince Edward Island Railway but refused. Acquired by the Gowrie Coal Mining Co. in 1877.
B—Possibly not acquired until 1882. Ordered through J. R. Banks and originally named "*Formosa*"; later named "*Blowers P. Archibald*".

Locomotive No. 1, "St. Pie", of the Lake Champlain & Saint Lawrence Junction Railway, standing at the bridge over the Black River at its namesake town in 1879. Surnamed "La Petite Boule"—"the little (musket) ball"—No. 1 was the subject of an extensive mythology among the inhabitants of the Yamaska valley.

Scarcely a year later, early in 1881, the South Eastern system acquired control and changed the gauge of the railway and of its locomotives.

The Lake Champlain & St. Lawrence Junction Railway, due to its short and uneventful history, had few features to distinguish it. One of the exceptions was the 4-4-0 locomotive *"St. Pie"* (Kingston-built and similar to the Toronto & Nipissing *"Uxbridge"*)

which, surnamed "the little bullet" in the French language, was said to have been endowed with various powers of speed and endurance, few of which bear credence in the cold light of factual reportage. One can scarcely imagine the *"St. Pie"* speeding across the countryside from St. Guillaume to Farnham at an average speed in excess of sixty miles per hour, as was claimed!

Lake Champlain & Saint Lawrence Junction Railway Company

Farnham to Stanbridge, Que. .... 13.8 miles
Farnham to St. Guillaume, Que. .... 46.7   "

Gauge: 3 feet, 6 inches.

Chronology:

1871	—Incorporation of Philipsburg, Farnham & Yamaska Railway Company.
1875	—Name changed to Lake Champlain & Saint Lawrence Junction Railway Company.
1879, Oct.	—Opened for service from Stanbridge to St. Guillaume, Que.
1880	—Leased to South Eastern Railway Company. Gauge later changed to 4'8½".

Steam Locomotives

No.	Builder	Year	C/N	Type	Cyls.	Dri.	From	To			Notes
1	Canadian	1879		4-4-0	11½x18"	39"	New ?	SER	#19	1881	A
2	"	"		"	13 x18"	45"	"	"	#20	"	B
3	"	"		"	"	"	"	"	#21	"	C
4	"	"		"	13½x20"	52"	"	"	#22	"	D

Notes: A—Named *"St. Pie"*.
  B—Named *"Abbottsford"*.
  C—Named *"Bedford"*.
  D—Named *"L'Ange Gardien"*. When acquired by the South Eastern Railway in 1881, these locomotives were converted to 4'8½" gauge.

•9•
Newfoundland Railway

Newfoundland Railway Company (I)	1881-1888
Placentia Railway	1888-1890
Hall's Bay Railway	1890-1893
Newfoundland Northern and Western Railway	1893-1898
Newfoundland Railway (II)	1898-1901
Reid-Newfoundland Company	1901-1923
Newfoundland Government Railway	1923-1926
Newfoundland Railway (III)	1926-1949
Canadian National Railways	1949-1981
TerraTransport	1981-1988

WHEN THE NEWFOUNDLAND RAILWAY WAS chartered by the Government of that British colony (then separate politically from Canada) on May 9th 1881, the selection of the narrow gauge of 3'6" for this system was almost automatic, because of its economic characteristics. Until this time, the inhabitants of the oldest British Crown Colony (discovered in 1497) eked out a precarious existence on the shores of this huge island. The only means of communication was by coasting vessels, subject to the vagaries of the sea and weather. The tiny settlements in the coves and inlets had to be virtually self-sufficient, making fish, particularly the cod, the staple article of diet and economy alike, and even, at times, serving as currency.

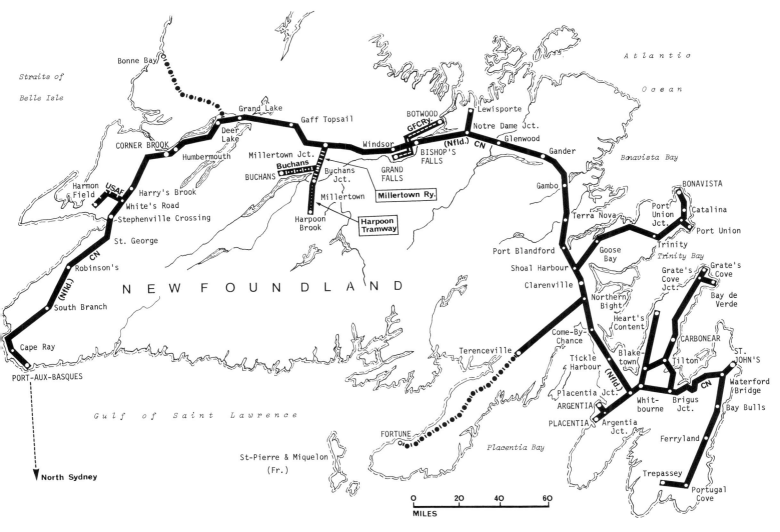

Barren countryside surrounding Carbonear, Newfoundland, acts as a backdrop for mixed train 212, headed by General Motors Diesel 875-hp units on June 20th 1967.

Train No. 2 "The Caribou", meets engine 902, heading a westbound freight at Harry's Brook, Newfoundland in June 1956. This was part of a four-way meet involving two passenger trains and two freight trains—a most uncommon feature of railroading in the tenth province where trains were short but frequent. The fireman on the second Mikado was Joseph Battiste.

Engineman Kevin Byrne leans out of the cab of No. 919 heading "The Caribou" near Cooke, Newfoundland, on June 20th 1967.

Nonetheless, there was a considerable forested area in the interior, particularly on the western half of the island, and mining would, in time, take an important place among the industries of Newfoundland.

Accordingly, in 1881, a terminus was selected in St. John's near the site of old Fort William, practically where now stands the Newfoundland Hotel of the Fairmont group. The rails headed out in an easterly direction, made a counter-clockwise half circle, turning westward toward the Blackmarsh Valley on the rocky heights above the old city. A short distance to the west, at Topsail, it crossed the rocky backbone of

the Avalon Peninsula and descended to the beach at Holyrood on Conception Bay. The line was completed to Holyrood in July 1882, and by the fall of that year, reached Salmon Cove.

The railway was headed toward Carbonear, also on Conception Bay, nearly one hundred miles away. Early in 1884, while work on the railway was still in progress, a regular service was started between St. John's and Holyrood, where a steamer connected to Brigus, Bay Roberts, Harbour Grace and Carbonear. In November 1884, the railway was finally completed after severe financial vicissitudes, to Harbour Grace

In a scene reminiscent of the 1920s and '30s, passengers are seated on the rear platform of an open observation car on the westbound "Caribou" enroute from St. John's to Port-aux-Basques in the summer of 1956. The car was one of three such open vestibule cars in operation at the time.

by way of Whitbourne and Tilton. This railway was officially a private company, but it carried on the construction largely with money borrowed on bond issues, and on government guarantees and subsidies. After the completion of the railway to Harbour Grace, it failed, and its assets were taken over by the Newfoundland Government.

In 1886, the Government itself started work on a railway from the Newfoundland Railway at Whitbourne, to the port of Placentia; this railway, known as the Placentia Railway, was opened on October 2nd 1888. This construction proved to be costly, so much so that the Government decided to ask for tenders for construction from outside contractors on future projects of this kind.

Upon the completion of the Placentia Railway, the Government decided to extend the railway to Hall's Bay, on Notre Dame Bay, about 280 miles from Whitbourne. Accordingly, the Placentia Railway was included as part of a new railway, called the Hall's Bay

Railway, and when contracts for construction were awarded, the successful bidder was Mr. (later Sir) Robert G. Reid, of Montreal. The contract was signed in 1890 and in the ensuing three years, the railway was built up the eastern side of the Island, reaching Norris Arm in 1893. At this point, the plans were changed to provide for the western terminal at Port-aux-Basques, instead of Hall's Bay, and it was under the title of a third company, the Newfoundland Northern & Western Railway, that the line was finally completed to Port-aux-Basques, 547 miles from St. John's, in 1897.

While the road was under construction, Mr. Reid, the contractor, entered into a contract with the Government, under which he agreed to operate the railway for ten years from September 1st 1893, in return for a grant of 5,000 acres of land for each mile of line operated. In 1898, following completion of the railway to Port-aux-Basques, Reid negotiated a further contract to operate the railway for fifty years, on certain

J. A. BROWN

Observation-platform-equipped sleeping car "Fogo" of Canadian National's Newfoundland lines, pictured at St. John's in June 1967.

conditions. The new system included all of the Government-built lines, now incorporated in the Newfoundland Northern & Western Railway, as well as the erstwhile private company, the (first) Newfoundland Railway Company. The new amalgamated railway was a proprietorship called simply "Newfoundland Railway". In 1901, Robert Reid incorporated under the name Reid-Newfoundland Company and all the rolling stock was so lettered.

The formal opening of the trans-insular railway took place when the first regular train left St. John's at 7 pm on Wednesday, June 29th 1898 and arrived at Port-aux-Basques at 10:45 pm on the following day, taking 27 hours and 45 minutes for the 547-mile run. During the run, seven locomotives were used in relays, the types including 4-4-0s, 4-6-0s and a 2-6-0.

The year 1898 also saw the construction of the Lewisporte branch, the "cut-off" from Brigus Junction to Tilton, and the extension from Harbour Grace to Carbonear. Ten years elapsed before further

thought was given to branch lines, but between 1911 and 1915, another intensive spurt of branch building resulted in the construction of lines to Bonavista, Trepassey, Heart's Content, Grates Cove and Bay-de-Verde. Another branch was started from Northern Bight to Fortune, but it was completed only as far as Terrenceville. Another line was projected from Deer Lake to Bonne Bay, but it never progressed beyond a partially-graded stage.

In 1920, the Reid-Newfoundland Company got into financial difficulties as a result of the extensive branch-line building, and following an appeal for aid to the Government, the latter hired Mr. R. C. Morgan of the Canadian Pacific Railway, to act as "general manager"—a liaison position between the Reid Company and the railway. This arrangement lasted only for a short time, and on the heels of a dispute which arose in 1922 between the Government and the Reid-Newfoundland Company, the government, on July 1st 1923, repossessed the railway and started

Pacific type (4-6-2) locomotive 599 was photographed switching the yard at Carbonear on June 21st 1956. It was preparing to turn on the wye in order to handle the mixed train back to St. John's. Note the stub switches which were replaced following dieselization.

to operate it as the "Newfoundland Government Railway". In 1926, an Act was passed changing the name of the railway to the "Newfoundland Railway".

During the 1930s, many of the impulsively-built branch lines were abandoned. These curtailments did away with the branches to Terrenceville, Trepassey, Hearts Content, Grates Cove and Bay-de-Verde. The remaining system, consisting of a main line from St. John's to Port-aux-Basques, with branches from Brigus Junction to Carbonear; from Placentia Junction to Argentia and Placentia; Shoal Harbour to Bonavista; and Notre Dame Junction to Lewisporte, is the same system which, in 1949, upon Newfoundland's confederation with Canada, became a part of the Canadian National Railways system. The resulting 700-mile narrow gauge network, dieselized and modernized, formed North America's largest concentration of narrow gauge railways.

The effect on railway traffic of the Trans-Canada Highway across Newfoundland was profound. Newer, much larger ferries linking Nova Scotia and Newfoundland entered service. These could handle tractor-trailers for freight, although some could handle rail cars as well. This latter feature gave rise to the concept of transferring the standard gauge car bodies onto narrow gauge trucks for rail movement across the island. This operation was performed at a facility

Carbonear-bound mixed train takes siding at Avondale for the eastbound "Caribou", in June 1952.

constructed for the purpose at Port-aux-Basques. While this eliminated the inefficiency of transshipping all freight to and from narrow gauge cars, it didn't lessen the effect of highway competition. Indeed, TerraTransport itself sponsored highway services.

In 1965, some standard gauge track was constructed at Port-aux-Basques to enable standard gauge cars to be moved to that point from the mainland, placed alongside narrow gauge equipment, and cargo transshipped once rather than the previous double transshipment of car-to-ship; ship-to-car.

Further economies were required, and in 1968 preliminary work commenced on the concept of transferring standard gauge cars onto narrow gauge trucks for movement in Newfoundland. This was in full operation by 1970.

This concept was not confined to specialized equipment. Cars of other railways were also retrucked in this manner, and as a result Canadian Pacific cars, for example, could be found travelling on the narrow gauge rails.

Of course, it was necessary to have a train ferry to handle such cars between the mainland and Newfoundland. Accordingly, a stern-loading vessel, the *"Frederick Carter"*, was constructed for the purpose. She entered service in 1968 and handled standard gauge cars to and from Port-aux-Basques as described. At that time such cars were transshipped at that point.

Inevitably the railway operation went into a decline. By the mid-1980s, it was obvious that the

Newfoundland Railway locomotive 1024, Mikado Type (2-8-2), is seen at the head end of a trans-island train at the station at St. John's in 1949. This engine was built by Montreal Locomotive Works in that year, subsequently renumbered 324 and scrapped in 1957. In this view, the conductor and engineer are verifying their train orders before departing for Port-aux-Basques, Newfoundland.

Steam operation on the old Newfoundland Railway was in its final months when this photograph was taken. It is of westbound Train No. 1 "Caribou" passing over the Main River at Stephenville Crossing, Newfoundland on June 24th 1956. Locomotives 312 and 317 were doing the honours on that day.

Doubleheaded Mikados headed by locomotive 320 were hauling the westbound "Caribou" when they paused for water at the double-spouted tank at Brigus Junction, Newfoundland. This was in the summer of 1956 when steam operation was in its decline on the island. No. 320 was scrapped the following year.

Canadian National 2-8-2s Nos. 323 and 314 heading No. 2 "The Caribou", eastbound, with a consist of twelve passenger cars, take water at Codroy Pond, Newfoundland on June 19th 1956.

The shop yard at St. John's, Newfoundland, as it appeared one winter's day during World War II. Locomotives are old 2-8-0s and 4-6-0s out of service, dating back to Reid-Newfoundland days. Body of baggage car at left, long a familiar sight at this location, is reputedly that of the first such car to cross Newfoundland when service was inaugurated in 1897.

railway would not survive. Finally, at the end of September 1988, the railway closed and by the end of 1990 the rails had been removed. Sometime after the turn of the century, the location of the station in St. John's was changed from the site of Fort William, to the location at the head of the harbour, where the railway also had its yards and repair shops.

The station building accommodated the headquarters offices of the railway, as well as the travelling public. With the demise of the railway, its future was uncertain until late in 2001 when the City of St. John's purchased it. It is believed to be intended to house a railway and coastal steamship museum.

The rolling stock was always particularly interesting, and possessed pleasing idiosyncrasies. One of the most distinctive practices, redolent of European railways, was the painting of the end of the steam locomotive buffer beams in crimson. At one time, too, the railway operated a bustling commuter service out of St. John's, using British-built Sentinel steam cars.

Canadian National's train No. 2 "Caribou" approaching Harry's Brook in June 1956.

R. J. Sandusky

R. J. Sandusky

A feature of the Newfoundland Railway was the configuration of the track as it followed the undulating landscape. These two views of the second-to-last eastbound "Caribou", with engines 907 and 935, clearly demonstrate this. Taken on June 29th 1969, the upper photograph was just north of Wreck House while the lower was between St. Andrew's and Doyle's.

August 25th 1975 saw a work stoppage by locomotive engineers with the result that the weekly mixed train from Bonavista, Newfoundland was the only revenue movement on the Island that day. Here that very low revenue train, hauled by engine 804, is seen rounding the top end of Trinity Harbour, Newfoundland.

Stub switches were a common feature on branch lines in Newfoundland. Here engine 804 pauses at Port Rexton with its mixed train from Bonavista on August 25th 1975.

J. A. BROWN

Interior of Canadian National's Newfoundland shop at St. John's, June 1967.

R. J. SANDUSKY

The last train No. 102 "Caribou" featured three diesel units and sixteen cars as it departed from Stephenville Crossing on July 2nd 1969. Besides a steam generator car, the train had one baggage/express car, four coaches, two dining cars and eight sleeping cars. The diesel units were 923, 910 and 906.

Train 401, headed by GMDL-built units 913, 904, 925 holds the main line at a 1967 meet at Kelligrews, Newfoundland, the locale of a fabled event commemorated in Newfoundland song and folklore, the "Kelligrews Soiree".

Opposite upper: GMDL-built diesels 919 and 911 are the head-end of "The Caribou" in this photograph taken at Cooke during June 1967.

Opposite lower: Three Canadian National 875-hp diesel units, Nos. 804, 800 and 801, stand on siding opposite St. John's station on June 22nd 1967. Railway shop building, in which Reid-Newfoundland Company built steam locomotives more than half a century before, stands in background.

J. A. BROWN

J. A. BROWN

An unusual official car owned by the Newfoundland Railway was the aptly-titled "Business Car", whose lounge area was graced by a picture window four feet wide. The car is pictured at St. John's in June 1952; it was scrapped shortly afterward.

OMER LAVALLÉE

The last observation cars operated on long-distance trains in North America were to be seen on the Newfoundland lines of Canadian National Railways through the 1960s. The cars were eight-section, one drawing room "standard" sleeping cars in other respects. The "Grand Falls", shown here at St. John's in 1952, was an older car. Later versions had arched roofs.

OMER LAVALLÉE

The former Newfoundland Railway had a considerable variety of "cabin cars" or cabooses, ranging from the more conventional cupola-topped cars to former passenger cars, such as No. 6009, shown here in Canadian National colours. The photograph was taken west of Harbour Grace, Newfoundland in 1967.

J. A. BROWN

The flat and barren terrain along much of the Newfoundland Railway's route caused problems with wind and snow. The line maintained a considerable fleet of wedge plows, backed up by three rotary plows, such as Canadian National No. 3650, shown here at Humbermouth, Newfoundland in June 1956.

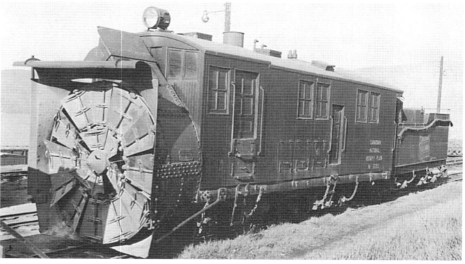

R. J. SANDUSKY

Wood-sheathed truss-rodded boxcars were a common sight on Newfoundland lines in the 1950s.

The Newfoundland Railway logo and slogan were featured on this outside-frame box car #2366. This car was built in October 1942 and was photographed at Bishop's Falls, Newfoundland in July 1943. These cars were used for general merchandise.

Standard gauge car mounted on 42"-gauge trucks looks incongruous coupled to normal Newfoundland equipment. This CN procedure is reminiscent of former similar practice of East Broad Top Railroad in Pennsylvania where standard gauge hopper cars were placed on 36"-gauge trucks.

Newfoundland Railway (1881-1897)
Southern Division—so-called "Harbour Grace Railway"
Northern Division—so-called "Placentia Railway" (1886-1890)
"Halls Bay Railroad" (1890-1894)
"Newfoundland Northern & Western Railway" (1894-1897)
Reid-Newfoundland Company (1897-1923)
Newfoundland Government Railway (1923-1926)
Newfoundland Railway (1926-1949)
Canadian National Railways/TerraTransport (1949-1988)

St. John's (Fort William) to Western Junction	8.0 miles	aban.	
Western Jct. to Whitbourne	47.5	"	"
Whitbourne to Blaketown	4.0	"	"
Blaketown to Tilton	12.5	"	"
Tilton to Harbour Grace	6.0	"	"
Whitbourne to Placentia	24.5	"	"
Placentia Junction to Norris Arm	192.3	"	"
Norris Arm to Port-aux-Basques	294.0	"	"
Brigus Junction to Tilton	26.5	"	"
Notre Dame Junction to Lewisporte	9.4	"	"
Harbour Grace to Carbonear	6.0	"	"
Western Junction to St. John's (present station)	7.0	"	"

Shoal Harbour to Bonavista	87.9 miles	aban.	
Port Union Junction to Port Union	2.0	"	"
Waterford Bridge to Trepassey	104.0	"	"
Blaketown to Heart's Content	39.0	"	"
Carbonear to Bay de Verde	48.0	"	"
Grates Cove Junction to Grates Cove	4.2	"	"
Goobies to Terrenceville (never operated)	42.0	"	"
Argentia Junction to Argentia	3.2	"	"

The following sections were started but not completed:

Terrenceville to Fortune	69.0	"
Grand Lake to Bonne Bay	38.0	"

Gauge: 3 feet, 6 inches.

Chronology:

1881, June 1 —Incorporation of the Newfoundland Railway Company to build from St. John's to Harbour Grace (Southern Division) and from Whitbourne to Halls Bay (Northern Division).

1884, Nov. —Southern Division, known as "Harbour Grace Railway" completed from St. John's (Fort William) to Harbour Grace.

1888, Oct. 2 —Northern Division, known as "Placentia Railway" completed from Whitbourne to Placentia. (commenced in 1886).

1893 —Northern Division, now known as "Halls Bay Railroad" completed from Placentia Junction to Norris Arm (Exploits).

1897, autumn —Northern Division, now known as "Newfoundland Northern & Western Railway", completed from Norris Arm to Port-aux-Basques.

1898 —Reid-Newfoundland Company, incorporated in 1893, takes over operation of Northern and Southern Divisions of Newfoundland Railway Company.

1898, June 30 —First through train from St. John's arrives at Port-aux-Basques at 2245, having taken 27 hours 45 minutes for journey.

1898 —Lines completed from Notre Dame Junction to Lewisporte, from Harbour Grace to Carbonear and from Brigus Junction to Tilton. Line from Blaketown to Tilton abandoned.

1899 —Line commenced from Western Junction to existing terminal at head of St. John's harbour but opened only in January 1903, at which time old Fort William terminal and connecting line abandoned.

1910 —Grand Lake to Bonne Bay line authorized, but never completed. *

1911, Nov. 8 —Opening of Shoal Harbour–Bonavista branch, commenced 1909. *

1911 —Opening of Port Union Junction–Port Union branch.

1914, Jan. 1 —Opening of Waterford Bridge–Trepassey branch, commenced 1911. *

1915, July —Opening of Blaketown–Heart's Content branch, commenced 1914, also extension from Carbonear to Bay de Verde, commenced 1913. *

1915, Oct. 11 —Opening of Grates Cove branch, commenced 1913. *

1915 —Fortune line commenced from Goobies to Fortune, but only 43 miles completed to Terrenceville and never operated. *

1921 —Argentia branch completed.

1921, May 16-23 —Railway operation ceased due to dispute between Reid-Newfoundland Company and government.

1923, July 1 —Reid-Newfoundland Company taken over by government and operated as Newfoundland Government Railway.

1926, June 9 —Original name, Newfoundland Railway, restored.

1934 —Trepassey, Bay de Verde and Grates Cove branches abandoned.

1939, June 1 —Unused Goobies–Terrenceville branch dismantled.

1939 —Whitbourne–Heart's Content branch abandoned.

1949, Mar. 31 —Newfoundland confederates with Canada, and Newfoundland Railway incorporated into Canadian National Railways.

1979 —Canadian National changes name of Newfoundland Division to TerraTransport.

1988, Sep. 30 —TerraTransport ceases railway operations.

* Extensions all authorized in 1910.

This builder's photograph reputedly illustrates the first locomotive used in Newfoundland. A comparison with the photograph on Page 56 suggests that it is more probable that it was a promotional photograph used by Hawthorn Leslie to promote their engines to the Blackman syndicate in 1881.

A.L.BLACKMAN

HUNSLET

Motive Power

Notes on Locomotive Rosters:

The lists are divided into four:

(a) Steam locomotives of the Southern Division of the Newfoundland Ry. (upper right);

(b) Steam locomotives of the Northern Division of the Newfoundland Ry. (lower right);

(c) Steam locomotives of the Reid-Newfoundland Company and its successors (see pages 57 & 61); and

(d) Internal combustion locomotives of the Newfoundland Railway and Canadian National Railways/TerraTransport (see page 63).

Lists (c) and (d) show two road number columns: that headed (1) is series in use until Canadian National Railways assumed control. List headed (2) is series devised and put into effect by CN in November 1950. It should be noted that CN locomotives 15-18 had numbers assigned but they were scrapped before these numbers applied. Locomotives shown as built by Reid-Newfoundland Company were built with parts supplied by Baldwin.

There is regrettably no information on individual scrapping dates for locomotives prior to 1949. In 1936, however, the following Newfoundland Railway locomotives were still in existence:

100 re#1; 107-109; 112-125; 151-153; 190-199; 1000-1003; — a total of 35 steam locomotives.

No. 100 re#1, built by Baldwin in 1898, was for many years assigned to yard service at St. John's and was known as "the Shunter". Only one ex-Newfoundland Railway steam locomotive has been preserved, No. 593, 4-6-2 type, in Lady Bowater Park, Corner Brook, Nfld.

Steam Locomotives
"Harbour Grace Railway" (1881-1898)
(Newfoundland Railway, Southern Division)

No.	Builder	Year	C/N	Type	Cyls.	Dri.	From	To		Notes
1	Haw.-Les.	1881	1884	0-6-0T	8x12"	27"	New	RNCo. #1	1898	A
2								" #2	"	
3								" #3	"	
4								" #4	"	
5								" #5	"	
6								" #6	"	
7	Haw.-Les.	1882	1885	2-6-0	13x18"	40"	New	RNCo. #20	1898	
8	"	"	1886	"	"	"	"	" #21	"	B
9	"	"	1887	"	"	"	"	" #22	"	
1/10	"	"	1888	"	"	"	"	x1887		
2/10	"	1888	2061	2-6-2	14x20"	42"	"	RNCo. #23	1898	
11	"	1882	1889	2-6-0	13x18"	40"	"	x1894		
12	Baldwin	1878	4345	"	14x18"	41"	NBR	X ?		C

> Some, if not all, of these were 4-4-0T Hunslet 1872, 10x16", 42" purchased from the Prince Edward Island Railway in 1881. Group may also have included one or more unaccounted locomotives from the New Brunswick Railway.

Notes:
A—RN #1 is displayed at the Mary March Museum, Grand Falls, Nfld.
B—Named "*St. Johns*".
C—#12 ex NBR #10. (q.v.)

Steam Locomotives
"Placentia Railway" (1886-1890);
"Halls Bay Railroad" (1890-1894);
"Newfoundland Northern & Western Railway" (1894-1898)
(Newfoundland Railway, Northern Division)

No.	Builder	Year	C/N	Type	Cyls.	Dri.	From	To		Notes
1	?	?	?	?	?	?	?			A
2	Baldwin	1889	10135	4-4-0	14x18"	48"	New	RNCo. #43	1898	
3	"	5/1891	11851	"	"	"	"	" #41	"	D
4	"	"	11859	2-6-0	16x20"	44"	"	" #60	"	
5	"	7/1891	12100	4-4-0	14x18"	48"	"	" #42	"	
6	"	6/1893	13519	2-6-0	16x20"	44"	"	" #61	"	
7	"	"	13518	4-4-0	14x18"	48"	"	" #40	"	
8	"	7/1893	13566	2-4-2T	"	44"	"	" # 8	"	
9	"	"	13567	"	"	"	"	" # 9	"	
10	"	3/1894	13968	0-4-2T	9x16"	33"	"	" #10	"	
11	"	"	13976	2-6-0	16x20"	44"	"	" #62	"	
12	"	4/1897	15308	4-6-0	"	"	"	" #1/105	"	B,Y
13	"	"	15309	"	"	"	"	" # 102	"	C

Notes:
A—No information available. Could have come from same group as Nos. 2-6 of "Harbour Grace Railway".
B—Named "*Sir Herbert Murray*".
C—Named "*Hon. Robert Bond*".
D—Named "*Sir William V. Whiteway*".
Y—For simplification, the following is sequential life of Baldwin C/N 15308:

1897	New #12	Newfoundland Northern & Western.
1898	Re# 1/105	Newfoundland Railway (R. G. Reid Proprietor).
1900	Re# 109	Newfoundland Railway (R. G. Reid Proprietor).
1901	Became #1/109	Reid-Newfoundland Company.
1908	Re# 209	Reid-Newfoundland Company.
1917	Re# 3/105	Reid-Newfoundland Company.
1928	Retired	

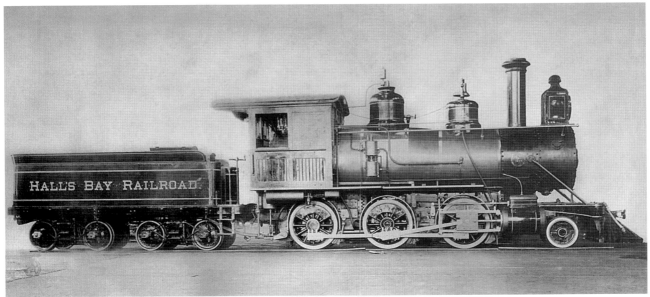

BALDWIN LOCOMOTIVE WORKS

Hall's Bay Railroad 2-6-0 No. 4 was built by the Baldwin Locomotive Works of Philadelphia, Pennsylvania.

The first locomotive to arrive in Newfoundland in 1881 was "Harbour Grace Railway" No. 1, built by Hawthorn Leslie in England. It ended up on the AND Co.'s Botwood Railway and is shown here, derelict, at Grand Falls, Newfoundland in the late 1930s just prior to being scrapped.

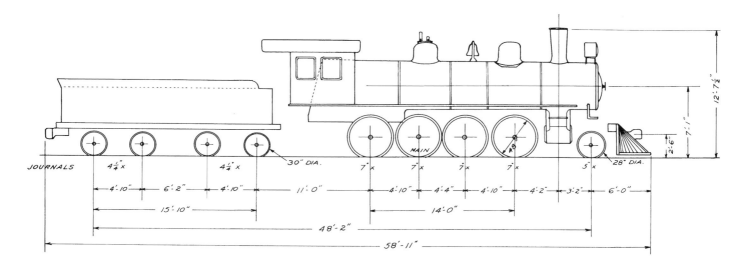

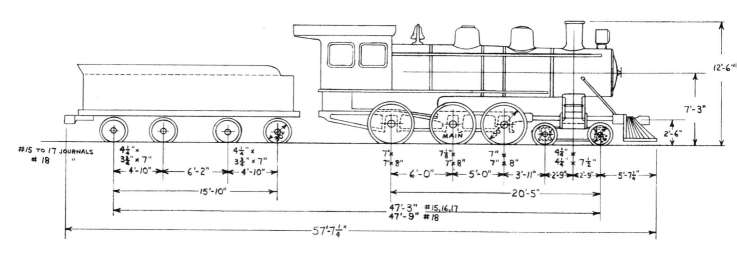

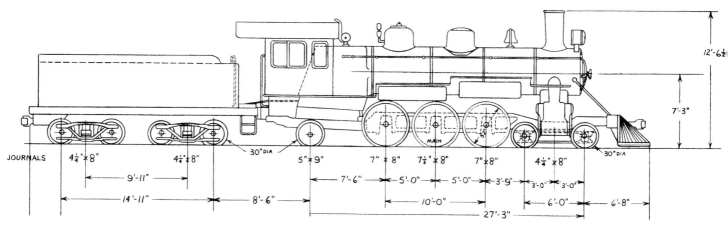

Steam Locomotives
Reid-Newfoundland Company (1898-1923);
Newfoundland Government Railway (1923-1926);
Newfoundland Railway (1926-1949);
Canadian National Railways (1949-1979)

Nos. (1)	(2)	Builder	Year	C/N	Type	Cyls.	Dri.	From	CN Class	To	Notes
1/1		Haw.-Les.	1881	1884	0-6-0T	8x12"	27"	HGR #1 1898		Bot. #1 1898	
2/1		Baldwin	1898	16244	4-6-0	16x20"	44"	#100 1925		x6/1939	
2										x1889	
3										x1891	
4										x1891	
5										x1891	
6										x1893	
8		Baldwin	7/1893	13566	2-4-2T	14x18"	44"	NN&W	#8 1898	x1925	
9		"	"	13567	"	"	"	"	#9 "	x1934	
10		"	3/1894	13968	0-4-2T	9x16"	33"	"	#10 "	Intl. P&P#1 19?	
20		Haw.-Les.	1882	1885	2-6-0	13x18"	42"	HGR	#7 "		
21		"	"	1886	"	"	"	"	#8 "	x	
22		"	"	1887	"	"	"	"	#9 "	x	
23		"	1888	2061	2-6-2	14x20"	"	"	#10 "	x	
40		Baldwin	6/1893	13518	4-4-0	14x18"	48"	NN&W	#7 "	x	
41		"	5/1891	11851	"	"	"	"	#3 "	x	
42		"	7/1891	12100	"	"	"	"	#5 "	x	
43		"	1889	10135	"	"	"	"	#2 "	Bot. #8 1918	
60		"	5/1891	11859	2-6-0	16x20"	44"	"	#4 "	x	
61		"	6/1893	13519	"	"	"	"	#6 "	x	
62		"	3/1894	13976	"	"	"	"	#11 "	x	
100		"	10/1898	16244	4-6-0	"	"	"	New		re#1 1925	
101		"	"	16245	"	"	"	"	"		x	
102		"	4/1897	15309	"	"	"	"	NN&W	#13 1898	x	
103		"	10/1898	16271	"	"	"	"	New		x	
104		"	"	16272	"	"	"	"	"		x	
1/105		"	4/1897	15308	"	"	"	"	NN&W	#12 1898	re#1/109 1900	Y
2/105		"	2/1900	17510	"	"	"	"	New		re#125 1918	Z
3/105		"	4/1897	15308	"	"	"	"	RNCo.	#209	x 1928	Y
106		"	2/1900	17511	"	"	"	"	New		x	A
107		"	6/1900	17832	"	"	"	"	"		x 1939	
108		"	"	17837	"	"	"	"	"		x	
1/109		"	4/1897	15308	"	"	"	"	RNCo.	#1/105	re#209 1908	Y
2/109		"	1/1908	32576	"	17x22"	50"	New			x 1939	
110		"	"	32577	"	"	"	"	"		x	
111		RNCo.	1911	1	"	"	"	"	"		x	
112		"	"	2	"	"	"	"	"		x	
113	(15)	"	1912	3	"	"	"	"	F-3-a	x 12/51	
114	(16)	"	"	4	"	"	"	"	"	x 12/51	
115		"	1913	5	"	"	"	"		x by 1938	
116		"	"	6	"	"	"	"		x 1938	
117	(17)	"	1914	7	"	"	"	"	F-3-a	x 7/53	
118		"	"	8	"	"	"	"		x 1938	
119		"	1915	9	"	"	"	"		x	
120		"	"	10	"	"	"	"		x	
121		Baldwin	10/1917	46636	"	"	"	"		x 1938	
122	(18)	"	"	46637	"	"	"	"	F-3-a	x 7/53	
123		"	"	46638	"	"	"	"		x 1939	
124		"	"	46691	"	"	"	"		x	
125		"	2/1900	17510	"	16x20"	"	Ex 2/105		x 1939	Z
150		"	2/1903	21597	2-8-0	18x24"	48"	New		x 1934	
151		"	"	21598	"	"	"	"		x	
152	280	RNCo.	1916	11	"	"	"	"	L-5-a	x 4/55	
153		"	"	12	"	"	"	"		x	
190	590	Baldwin	1920	54398	4-6-2	17x24"	52"	"	J-8-a	x 4/57	
191	591	"	"	54399	"	"	"	"	"	x 4/57	
192	592	"	"	54400	"	"	"	"	"	x 4/57	
193	593	"	"	54401	"	"	"	"	"	Preserved 11/58	
194	594	"	"	54466	"	"	"	"	"	x 8/58	
195	595	"	"	54467	"	"	"	"	"	x 4/57	
196	596	"	1926	59531	"	18x24"	"	"	J-8-b	x 3/57	
197	597	Montreal	"	67129	"	"	"	"		x 4/57	
198	598	Alco	1929	67941	"	"	"	"	J-8-c	Bot. #598 3/57	
199	599	"	"	67942	"	"	"	"	"	" #599 "	
209		Baldwin	4/1897	15308	4-6-0	16x20"	44"	RNCo.	#1/109	re#3/105 1917	Y

> See comments under same numbers, "Harbour Grace Railway" (see page 55). One possibly sold to Millertown Railway instead of being scrapped, as noted.

Notes: A—C/N also given as 17831.

Y—For simplification, the following is sequential life of Baldwin C/N 15308:

1897	New #12	Newfoundland Northern & Western.
1898	Re# 1/105	Newfoundland Railway (R. G. Reid Proprietor).
1900	Re# 109	Newfoundland Railway (R. G. Reid Proprietor).
1901	Became #1/109	Reid-Newfoundland Co.
1908	Re# 209	Reid-Newfoundland Co.
1917	Re# 3/105	Reid-Newfoundland Co.
1928	Retired

Z—For simplification, the following is sequential life of Baldwin C/N 17510:

1900	New #2/105	Newfoundland Railway (R. G. Reid Proprietor).
1901	Became #105	Reid-Newfoundland Co.
1917	Re# 125	Reid-Newfoundland Co.
1939	Retired.

Steam Locomotives 1000-1029
are listed on page 61

NEWFOUNDLAND RAILWAY 2-8-0

Road Nos.	152
Gauge	42"
Type	2-8-0
Builder	REID
Date	1912
Cylinders (diam. & stroke)	18"x22"
Driving Wheels	48"
Pressure	180 p.s.i.
Tractive Effort	22,720 lbs.

Weights (working order)

On drivers	125,660 lbs.
Total engine	146,600 lbs.
Tender	80,000 lbs.

Tender Capacity

Coal	8 tons
Water	2,400 gals.
Oil	—

NEWFOUNDLAND RAILWAY 4-6-0

Road Nos.	122
Gauge	42"
Type	4-6-0
Builder	BLW
Date	1917
Cylinders (diam. & stroke)	17"x22"
Driving Wheels	50"
Pressure	180 p.s.i.
Tractive Effort	19,455 lbs.

Weights (working order)

On drivers	72,700 lbs.
Total engine	92,100 lbs.
Tender	56,000 lbs.

Tender Capacity

Coal	8 tons
Water	2,400 gals.
Oil	—

NEWFOUNDLAND RAILWAY 4-6-2

Road Nos.	190-195
Gauge	42"
Type	4-6-2
Builder	BLW
Date	1920
Cylinders (diam. & stroke)	17"x24"
Driving Wheels	52"
Pressure	180 p.s.i.
Tractive Effort	20,408 lbs.

Weights (working order)

On drivers	78,000 lbs.
Total engine	115,000 lbs.
Tender	84,000 lbs.

Tender Capacity

Coal	—
Water	3,000 gals.
Oil	1,665 gals.

Newfoundland Railway No. 108, a 4-6-0 built by Baldwin Locomotive Works.

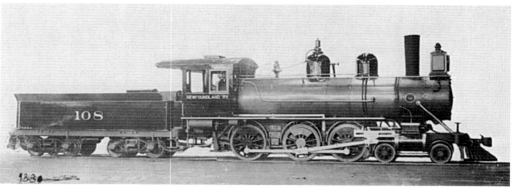

Newfoundland Railway No. 1, an ancient 4-6-0, was known popularly, but unofficially, as "The Shunter", because of its permanent assignment as the terminal yard engine in the Newfoundland capital. The unusual signal at the left—a semaphore blade in a "sandwich" made up of two glass discs—was for long the only fixed signal, apart from order boards, on the Island.

Aptly numbered 2-8-0 No. 280, bearing Newfoundland Railway's insignia but Canadian National number as Port-aux-Basques switcher, was the only coal-burning steam locomotive on the roster in 1952 when this photograph was made. It was built at St. John's in 1916 by Reid-Newfoundland Company using many components supplied by Baldwin.

The Baldwin Locomotive Works of Philadelphia, Pennsylvania outshopped Newfoundland Railway 4-6-2 No. 197.

Locomotive No. 193, later renumbered 593 by the CNR, was the first and last Pacific type to be operated in Newfoundland, in 1920 and November 1958 respectively. It is on static display at Corner Brook.

The turntable at Bishop's Falls was the locale of this June 30th 1943 view of Newfoundland Railway engine #190. This Pacific type (4-6-2) was built by Baldwin in 1920, renumbered 590 by Canadian National, and scrapped in 1957.

PATERSON-GEORGE COLLECTION; COURTESY COO-WEST COLLECTION #NF14

No. 594 handled switching duties at Port-aux-Basques in June 1956.

OMER LAVALLÉE

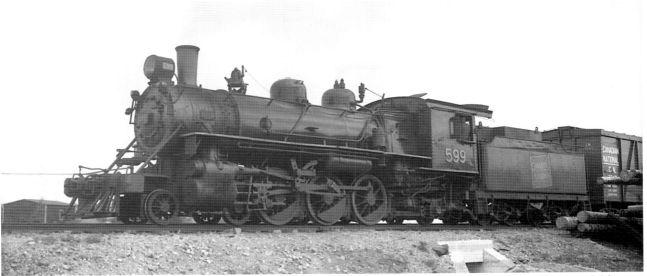

R. J. SANDUSKY

Engine 599, with Carbonear mixed train, is in the siding at Avondale to meet an eastbound freight on June 21st 1956.

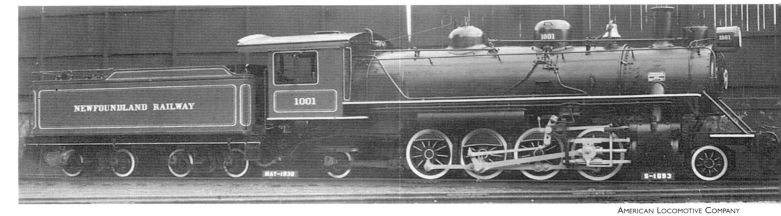

Newfoundland 2-8-2 No. 1001, later Canadian National No. 301, was constructed at Schenectady by American Locomotive Company in 1930.

Newfoundland Railway No. 1001, built by Alco in 1930, in pre-CN livery during the 1930s.

Newfoundland motive power in pre-CN livery at St. John's in the 1930s. No. 1003 was built by North British Locomotive Works in 1935.

No. 1021 was a 2-8-2 built by Montreal Locomotive Works for the Newfoundland Railway.

Steam Locomotives (continued from page 57)

Nos. (1)	(2)	Builder	Year	C/N	Type	Cyls.	Dri.	From	CN Class	To	Notes
1000	300	Alco	1930	68400	2-8-2	18x24"	48"	New	R-2-a	x 6/57	
1001	301	"		68401	"	"	"	"	"	x 3/57	
1002	302	No. Brit.	1935	24297	"	"	"	"	R-2-b	x 5/57	
1003	303	"		24298	"	"	"	"	"	x 9/57	
1004	304	"	1937	24436	"	"	"	"	"	x 3/57	
1005	305	"	1938	24521	"	"	"	"	"	x 11/57	
1006	306	"	"	24522	"	"	"	"	"	x 3/57	
1007	308	Montreal	1941	69444	"	"	"	"	R-2-c	Bot. #308 4/57	
1008	307	No. Brit.	"	24667	"	"	"	"	R-2-b	x 5/57	
1009	309	Alco	"	69736	"	"	"	"	R-2-c	x 5/57	
1010	310	"	"	69737	"	"	"	"	"	x 5/57	
1011	311	"	"	69738	"	"	"	"	"	x 5/57	
1012	312	"	"	69739	"	"	"	"	"	x 3/57	
1013	313	"	"	69740	"	"	"	"	"	x 6/57	
1014	314	Montreal	1941	69695	"	"	"	"	"	x 11/57	
1015	315	"	"	69696	"	"	"	"	"	x 6/57	
1016	316	Alco	1944	71963	"	"	"	"	"	x 8/57	
1017	317	"	"	71964	"	"	"	"	"	x 7/57	
1018	318	"	"	71965	"	"	"	"	"	x 7/57	
1019	319	"	"	71966	"	"	"	"	"	x 9/57	
1020	320	Montreal	1947	75635	"	"	"	"	R-2-d	x 7/57	
1021	321	"	"	75636	"	"	"	"	"	x 11/57	
1022	322	"	"	75637	"	"	"	"	"	x 10/57	
1023	323	"	"	75638	"	"	"	"	"	x 7/57	
1024	324	"	1949	76333	"	"	"	"	"	x 8/57	
1025	325	"	"	76424	"	"	"	"	"	x 9/57	
1026	326	"	"	76425	"	"	"	"	"	x 8/57	
1027	327	"	"	76426	"	"	"	"	"	Bot. #327 4/57	
1028	328	"	"	76427	"	"	"	"	"	x 12/57	
1029	329	"	"	76428	"	"	"	"	"	x 11/57	

NEWFOUNDLAND RAILWAY 2-8-2

Road Nos.	1000-1001
Gauge	42"
Type	2-8-2
Builder	ALCO
Date	1930
Cylinders (diam. & stroke)	18"x24"
Driving Wheels	48"
Pressure	200 p.s.i.
Tractive Effort	27,540 lbs.

Weights (working order)

On drivers	115,000 lbs.
Total engine	146,000 lbs.
Tender	102,900 lbs.

Tender Capacity

Coal	—
Water	4,170 gals.
Oil	2,170 gals.

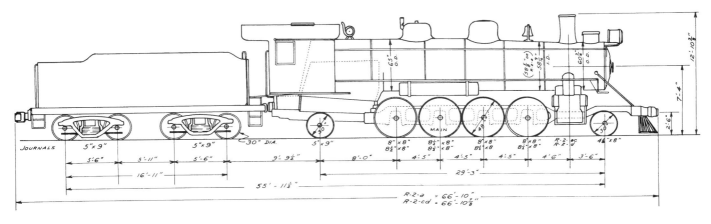

J. A. BROWN COLLECTION

Newfoundland Railway No. 1007 at Bishop's Falls, Newfoundland on June 30th 1943.

Before integration into Canadian National system after confederation with Canada in 1949, the Newfoundland Railway had experimented with diesel-electric yard engines. No. 775, formerly Newfoundland Railway No. 5000, which was built by General Electric at Erie, Pennsylvania in 1948, was photographed in St. John's yard in June 1952.

A General Electric shop photograph of Newfoundland Railway 380-hp switcher No. 5001. The engine is mounted on standard gauge carrying trucks. The three units of this series are now in Costa Rica, Central America.

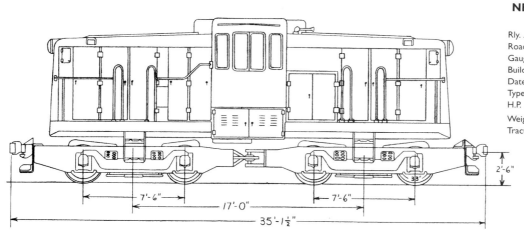

NEWFOUNDLAND RAILWAY
TYPE B-B

Rly.	Newfoundland Rly.
Road Nos.	5000-5002
Gauge	42"
Builder	General Electric
Date	Aug. 1948
Type	B-B
H.P.	380
Weight (working order)	97,800 lbs.
Tractive Effort (continuous)	13,000 lbs.

Steam Self-Propelled Cars

Five motor passenger cars built by Sentinel-Cammell of Great Britain. Two, Newfoundland Ry. "A" and "B" in 1925; three more, "C", "D" and "E" in 1927. Used in suburban services. Scrapped.

CANADIAN NATIONAL TYPE A1A-A1A

Rly.	Canadian National
Road Nos.	900-902
Gauge	42"
Builder	General Motors Diesel Ltd.
Date	1952
Type	A1A-A1A
H.P.	1,200
Weight (working order)	222,180 lbs.
Tractive Effort (continuous)	40,000 lbs.

Diesel Electric Locomotives
Newfoundland Railway (1926-1949);
Canadian National Railways (1949-1979)
TerraTransport (1979-1988)

No. (1)	(2)	Builder	Year	C/N	Type	H.P.	From	CN Class	To	Notes
5000	775	GE	1948	29722	B-B	380	New	ES-4-a	sold 10/68	A
5001	776	"	"	29723	"	"	"	"	"	A
5002	777	"	"	29724	"	"	"	"	"	A
	800	GMDL	1956	A923	C-C	875	"	GR-9-b		B
801	"	"	A924	"	"	"	"	"		B
802	"	"	A925	"	"	"	"	"		C
803	"	"	A926	"	"	"	"	"		D
804	"	"	A927	"	"	"	"	"		B
805	"	"	A928	"	"	"	"	"		E
900	"	1952	A303	"	1200	"	Y-4-a, then GR-12-a		B
901	"	"	A304	"	"	"	" " "		B
902	"	"	A305	"	"	"	"		B
903	"	1953	A435	"	"	"	Y-4-b, then GR-12-b		B
904	"	"	A436	"	"	"	"		B
905	"	"	A437	"	"	"	" " "		B
906	"	"	A438	"	"	"	"		B
907	"	"	A439	"	"	"	" " "		B
908	"	"	A440	"	"	"	" " "		B
909	"	1956	A897	"	"	"	GR-12-g		B
910	"	"	A898	"	"	"	"		F
911	"	"	A899	"	"	"	"		F
912	"	"	A900	"	"	"	"	x 4/57	G
913	"	"	A901	"	"	"	"		B
914	"	"	A902	"	"	"	"		A
915	"	"	A903	"	"	"	"		F
916	"	"	A904	"	"	"	"		B
917	"	"	A905	"	"	"	"		B
918	"	"	A906	"	"	"	"		F
919	"	"	A907	"	"	"	"		B
920	"	"	A908	"	"	"		x 4/57	G
921	"	"	A909	"	"	"	"		F
922	"	"	A910	"	"	"	"		I
923	"	"	A911	"	"	"	"		B
924	"	"	A912	"	"	"	"		J
925	"	"	A913	"	"	"	"		K
926	"	"	A914	"	"	"	"		F
927	"	"	A915	"	"	"	"		L
928	"	"	A916	"	"	"	"		I
929	"	"	A917	"	"	"	"		F
930	"	"	A918	"	"	"	"		P
931	"	"	A919	"	"	"	"		M
932	"	"	A920	"	"	"	"		P
933	"	"	A921	"	"	"	"		F
934	"	"	A922	"	"	"	"		O
935	"	1958	A1450	"	"	"	GR-12-p		B
936	"	"	A1451	"	"	"	"		K
937	"	"	A1452	"	"	"	"		H
938	"	1960	A1834	"	"	"	GR-12-x		I
939	"	"	A1835	"	"	"	"		I
940	"	"	A1836	"	"	"	"		P
941	"	"	A1837	"	"	"	"		I
942	"	"	A1838	"	"	"	"		I
943	"	"	A1839	"	"	"	"		L
944	"	"	A1840	"	"	"	"		F
945	"	"	A1841	"	"	"	"		F
946	"	"	A1842	"	"	"	"		I

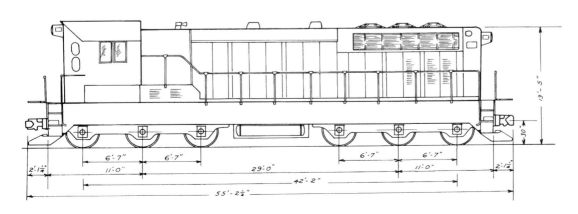

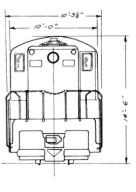

Although primarily known for its railway service, the Newfoundland Railway also operated a fleet of coastal vessels and a dry dock at St. John's. This photograph of the dry dock facility was taken by Ron Ritchie on June 26th 1952. In the foreground was the schooner "Maxwell F. Corkum" and, behind her, two other vessels.

Rather than an observation sleeping car, the last car on the eastbound Train No. 2, on June 25th 1952, was the standard sleeper "Buchans". The entire train was still in the red livery of the Newfoundland Railway. Note the smoke jacks for the Baker heaters (stoves) on these cars, as well as the baffles under certain windows. These were to deflect dust when the windows were open in hot weather (an infrequent occurrence in Newfoundland!).

Narrow gauge is evident as the main line crosses the Main River. The sandy soil is typical of that part of western Newfoundland.

Westbound freight train with a Mikado type locomotive is in the siding to meet Train No. 2 on June 25th 1952. The siding, in typical fashion on the island, runs behind the station building.

RON RITCHIE

Constant track maintenance was required in the harsh climate of Newfoundland. Here two work trains are at the Flat Bay ballast pit on June 19th 1956.

RON RITCHIE

Another view on the Carbonear Branch showing locomotive 599 with Train No. 7.

OMER LAVALLÉE

The roadbed of the Newfoundland Railway conformed to the undulating terrain as illustrated in this 1988 view.

Mixed train No. 7 was nearing Harbour Grace on June 21st 1956.

It was nearing the end of railway service when Omer Lavallée caught this lonely wayfreight. Adjacent is the Trans-Canada Highway which helped to accelerate the demise of the railway system..

Engine 599 hauls mixed train No. 7 near Spaniard's Bay June 21st 1956.

The consist of Train No. 2 for St. John's stands on the wharf at Port-aux-Basques on June 24th 1952. The baggage cars are being loaded at the shed behind the train and will be added before departure. The funnel of the steamer "Burgeo" which had just arrived from Sydney, Nova Scotia, can be seen behind the train.

CNR locomotive 303 is at the head end of Train No. 1 "The Caribou" as it prepares to depart from St. John's on June 26th 1952. Built by the North British Locomotive Works in 1935, the engine was scrapped in 1957.

Coaches on the Newfoundland Railway were of two varieties, first- and second-class. Here second-class coach No. 129 sits on a siding ready for the next assignment, probably on a branch line train, or to carry passengers locally on the rear of a freight train. This practice was common on the island where, at that time, roads were few and far between. Photo by the author June 25th 1952.

Westbound freight train pulls out of the siding after meeting train No. 2. The last car is a second-class coach, often provided to accommodate the locals who wish to travel short distances. Perhaps the two ladies have just disembarked from that train. Photo by the author on June 25th 1952.

Locomotive 300 heading Train No. 2 stands at a division point enroute from Port-aux-Basques to St. John's on June 25th 1952. As the train is being serviced, the blue flag signifying "Men At Work" (partially visible at right) has been attached to the rail in front of the engine. This meant that the train must not be moved until the flag has been removed.

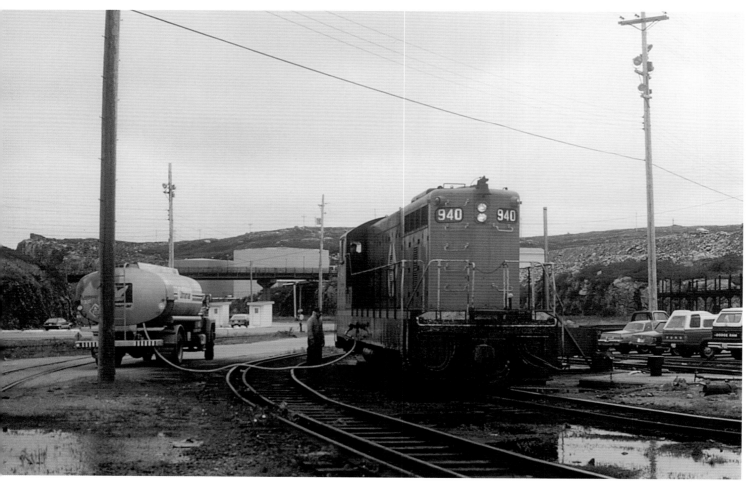

Diesel 940, bearing Terra Transport logo, is being refuelled in the summer of 1988. In the foreground is double gauge track that was used by standard gauge engines in loading and unloading the vessel from the mainland.

During the last years of operation, standard gauge freight cars were moved to Newfoundland and placed on narrow gauge trucks for movement on the island. Switching on and off the vessel that handled these cars was performed by a standard gauge diesel unit. In this photo taken in the summer of 1988, CN standard gauge engine 1766 is starting up with smoke typical of a steam engine. The nose of narrow gauge unit 940 is just visible to the right.

Consolidation type 2-8-0, appropriately numbered 280, and still bearing the Newfoundland Railway logo, was the yard switcher at Port-aux-Basques on June 24th 1952. This locomotive was built in the Reid-Newfoundland Company's shops in 1916 and was scrapped in April 1955.

Rail traffic was disrupted as a result of a derailment, which necessitated a three-way meet at Harry's Brook on June 19th 1956. Train No. 1, with engines 315 and 328 (shown opposite page, upper photo), is nose-to-nose with Extra 907 East (above). The views were taken by Ron Ritchie from the rear of Train No. 2.

A water standpipe of the type usually found on the Newfoundland Railway is depicted in this photograph taken by Omer Lavallée during his June 1952 visit to the island.

Other photographs taken on June 19th 1956 show congestion at meeting points resulting from a derailment near Harry's Brook. The clean up had not been completed when photographer Ron Ritchie passed that location.

In this photograph, taken in the summer of 1988, a freight train with passenger accommodation is seen passing a siding containing a snow plow ready for the next winter season. It was never used again, as the railway closed in September of that year.

NARROW GAUGE RAILWAYS OF CANADA

Several views taken by the author shortly before the end of railway service in Newfoundland.

OMER LAVALLÉE

OMER LAVALLÉE

An interesting "aerial" view of a short train with much power taken in the summer of 1988.

NARROW GAUGE RAILWAYS OF CANADA

RON RITCHIE

A pair of Newfoundland Railway snow plows were in the yard at Port-aux-Basques on June 24th 1952. One was a straight wedge plow for unmanned operation (no cupola), and the other was a single track plow with a cupola. This equipment was still in Newfoundland Railway colours.

OMER LAVALLÉE

The observation sleeping car "Fogo" brings up the rear of the trans-island passenger train in June 1952. This type of car was a not-unusual feature of these trains.

Even narrow gauge railways required the use of the auxiliary on occasion. The author photographed auxiliary crane No. 3352 at St. John's in the summer of 1988.

Mail car No. 231 was still in the red livery of the Newfoundland Railway when photographed at St. John's in June 1952.

Baggage car No. 223, in CNR livery, was photographed by the author in the yard at St. John's in June 1952. The narrow gauge equipment was in the process of being repainted in the Canadian National colour scheme.

Pacific type locomotive 599 was handling Mixed train No. 8 on the Carbonear Branch on June 21st 1956.

The editor and the author seem to have adopted a "possessive" stance in this photograph taken at Port-aux-Basques on June 24th 1952. The cars are refrigerator cars.

Freight train headed by engine 940 passes preserved locomotive 593 at Corner Brook in the late summer of 1988. Engine 940 itself was eventually preserved at Whitbourne.

No. 3732 was one of several brand new air dump cars that were in the yard at St. John's on June 26th 1952. Not only the condition of the paint indicated this, but the stencilling on the side stated "NEW 5-52".

Canadian National engine 775, one of the first group of diesels acquired by the Newfoundland Railway before confederation, stands in the yard at St. John's on a pleasant June day in 1952. Built by General Electric in 1948, this unit was sold in November 1968 to the Northern Railway of Costa Rica.

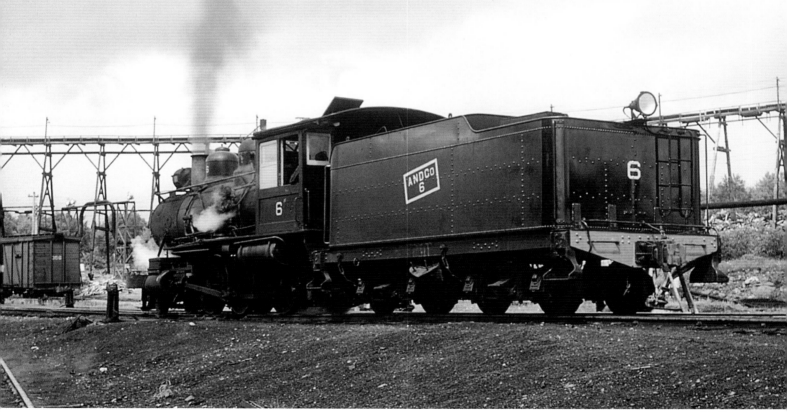

Anglo-Newfoundland Development Co. locomotive No. 6, a 4-6-0, is simmering gently at Grand Falls on June 28th 1952. It was built by Baldwin in 1917 and became Grand Falls Central No. 6 in 1957. It was scrapped in 1958.

10

Other Railways in Newfoundland

WHILE RAIL TRANSPORTATION IN THE Province of Newfoundland was dominated by the narrow gauge lines of the former Newfoundland Railway, possibly ten separate railways, at least, have existed in addition to the main-line services of the government railway, and for the purposes of convenience will all be treated here.

The majority of the independent mileage was the property of the Anglo-Newfoundland Development Company, and was divided into three systems, namely, the Millertown Railway, the Botwood Railway and the Harpoon Railway, (or Tramway).

The first section, constructed in 1901 by a lumberman named Miller, was a 19½ mile line from Millertown Junction, on the Newfoundland Railway, to Millertown. He sold the railway to the Newfoundland Timber Estates in 1902. The latter, in turn, sold the Millertown Railway to the Anglo-Newfoundland Development Co. (AND Co.) in 1910.

The first locomotive used by Miller on the Millertown Railway was No. 20, formerly Harbour Grace Railway No. 7. After a boiler explosion in 1897, this locomotive was rebuilt by the Reid interests in 1898, but did not operate satisfactorily. Miller complained and Reids replaced it with Hall's Bay Railway No. 43, which was the first locomotive bought by R. G. Reid for his Hall's Bay Railway. The sale of the Millertown Railway to the AND Co. included No. 43 which then became Botwood Railway No. 8.

At the time that the AND Co. acquired the Millertown Railway, it also secured the Mint Brook Tramway, a railway that connected Mint Brook and Gambo. Originally a wooden, or pole, railway using horses as motive power, it was later converted to steel rails. This line was built by J. J. Murphy, a Newfoundland lumberman who owned the telephone company in St. John's (later Newtel) and the electric company which became the Newfoundland Light & Power Co.

OMER LAVALLÉE

Buchans Railway (subsidiary of American Smelting & Refining Company) 4-6-0 No. 2 in the gloom of the Botwood Railway's shop at Botwood, Newfoundland in 1952.

AND Co. 2-6-2T No. 12 is standing in front of the Botwood Railway locomotive shop at Botwood on June 23rd 1956. Note the flanger mounted on the pilot truck frame.

The Botwood Railway's No. 9 was a dapper Baldwin 4-6-0, shown switching miniature boxcars at Botwood in June 1952.

AND Co. locomotive 10 (2-6-2T) switches beside the Botwood Railway station at Grand Falls, Newfoundland on June 23rd 1956.

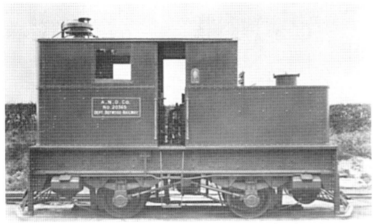

An unusual locomotive type for North America was the Botwood Railway's chain driven Sentinel steam locomotive, built in Great Britain. Newfoundland Railway also had five steam-driven Sentinel passenger motor cars.

Anglo-Newfoundland Development Company

Botwood Railway	Grand Falls to Botwood, Nfld.	22 miles	@GFC
	Grand Falls to (CNR) at Windsor, Nfld.	2 miles	@GFC
Millertown Railway	Millertown Junction to Millertown, Nfld.	19.5 miles	@part GFC
Harpoon Tramway	Millertown to Harpoon Brook, Nfld.	19 miles	aban.

Gauge: 3 feet, 6 inches.

Chronology:

1901	—Railway built from Millertown Junction on Newfoundland Railway, to Millertown, Nfld., by lumberman named Miller.
	—Anglo-Newfoundland Development Co. completes railway from paper mill at Grand Falls to ocean port of Botwood, Nfld.
1909	—AND Co. purchases Millertown Railway from Miller.
	—Millertown Railway extended from Millertown to Harpoon Brook for logging purposes; line known as Harpoon Tramway.
1928	—Buchans Mining Company (q.v.) connects its railway to Millertown Railway at Buchans Junction.
1957	—Harpoon Tramway and that part of Millertown Railway between Buchans Junction and Millertown abandoned.
1957, July 1	—Botwood Railway sold to new private company, Grand Falls Central Railway Company (q.v.).

Steam Locomotives

No.	Builder	Year	C/N	Type	Cyls.	Dri.	From	To	Notes
1	Baldwin	1907	31075	0-4-0T	12x17"	34"	New	GFC #1, 1957	
2	"	1909	33335	2-4-2T	12x16"	42"	"	x c1929	
3	"	"	33470	2-6-2T	17x22"	44"	"	x ?	
4	"	1910	34711	"	15x22"	"	"	x 1956	
5	"	1912	38184	"	"	"	"	x ?	
6	"	1917	45510	4-6-0	17x20"	50"	"	GFC #6, 1957	
7	Haw-Les.	1881	1884	0-6-0T	8x12"	27"	RNCo.# 1, 1918	x c1940	
8	Baldwin	1889	10135	4-4-0	14x18"	48"	RNCo.#43,1918	x ?	
9	"	1920	53253	4-6-0	17x20"	50"	New	GFC #9, 1957	
10	"	"	53503	2-6-2T	15x22"	44"	"	GFC #10, 1957	
11	"	"	53504	"	"	"	"	x ?	
12	"	1937	62137	"	16x22"	"	"	GFC #12, 1957	
14	No. Brit.	"	24437	2-8-2	18x24"	48"	"	GFC #14, 1957	
15	"	"	24438	"	"	"	"	GFC #15, 1957	
	Sentinel	1926	6416	- B -			"	x 1934	A

Notes: A—Road number of Sentinel steam locomotive is sometimes given as 20, but photo shows it lettered "Dept. Botwood Railway" with number 20365.

OMER LAVALLÉE

AND Co. locomotive No. 9 was photographed on June 23rd 1956. This 4-6-0 was built by Baldwin in 1920.

R. J. SANDUSKY

AND Co. (Millertown Railway) engine 23, a 14-Ton type JDTW Plymouth, is at the CNR station at Millertown Junction, Newfoundland on June 24th 1956. Joe Globe's Park is in the background. No. 23 is preserved at Trinity.

Steam Locomotives

In the independent period, 1901-09, the railway was presumably worked by an engine that was purchased from the Newfoundland Railway in 1900. This was #20, which was originally NF #7, a 2-6-0. (Hawthorn Leslie #1885). After 1909, trains were pulled by Newfoundland Railway locomotives and crews hired by AND Co. until advent of Buchans Railway traffic in 1928, after which NR engines used only occasionally.

Internal Combustion Locomotives

No.	Builder	Year	C/N	Type	Weight	H.P.	From	To	Notes
20	Whitcomb		12375	- B -			New?	x After 1956	DM
21				- B -					DM ,A
22	Vulcan	1930	4090	- B -			New	x 1956	GE
23	Plymouth	1952	5702	- C -			"	GFC #100, 1958	DTC

Notes: DM—Diesel-mechanical.

GE—Gas-electric.

DTC—Diesel torque converter.

A—No. 21 left at Exploits Dam when rails were lifted in 1958, along with flatcar to "ferry" trucks across dam. Disposition unknown.

The year 1909 saw the completion by the AND Co. of its Botwood Railway, from a paper mill at Grand Falls, through Bishop's Falls, to Botwood, situated on the Bay of Exploits, a distance of 22 miles. Some time subsequently the Millertown Railway was extended in a southerly direction some 19 miles into the bush to Lake Ambrose. This came to be known as the Harpoon Railway and was used principally for logging.

Buchans Mining Company Car No. 819 of a type known as a "covered wagon" was photographed at Botwood by Omer Lavallée on June 23rd 1956. These cars were used for mineral traffic.

In 1928, the Buchans Mining Company built a branch from the Millertown Railway at Buchans Junction, for 19 miles to Buchans.

All of these lines used a variety of steam locomotives which, in later years, gave way to diesel and gasoline engines.

While the Buchans Railway and that part of the Millertown Railway between Buchans Junction and Millertown Junction continued to be worked by the AND Co., the remaining sections of the Millertown Railway and the Harpoon Railway were dismantled in 1957. On July 1st of that year, the Botwood

J. A. BROWN

Nos. 5 and 6 of the Buchans Railway, Whitcomb products of 1949 and 1952, respectively, wait with a van at Millertown Junction, on June 23rd 1967.

American Smelting & Refining Company
(Buchans Mining Company)

Buchans Railway   Buchans Junction to Buchans, Nfld. .... 19 miles   @

Gauge: 3 feet, 6 inches.

Chronology:

1928 — Buchans Mining Company, a subsidiary of American Smelting & Refining Co., of the USA, builds railway from Buchans Junction on Millertown Railway to Buchans. Line known as Buchans Railway.

Steam Locomotives

No.	Builder	Year	C/N	Type	Cyls.	Dri.	From	To	Notes
1	Baldwin	1928	60378	2-4-2T	13x18"	42"	New	x ?	
2	"	1930	61252	4-6-0	17x22"	50"	"	x 195?	
3	Davenport	1936	2249	0-4-0T	8x12"	42"	"	x ?	

Internal Combustion Locomotives

No.	Builder	Year	C/N	Type	Weight	H.P.	From	To	Notes
4	Whitcomb	10/1949	61098	B-B	50 Ton	350	New		DE
5	"	"	61100	"	"	"	"		"
6	"	12/1952	61199	"	75 Ton	675	"		"

Notes: DE — Diesel-electric

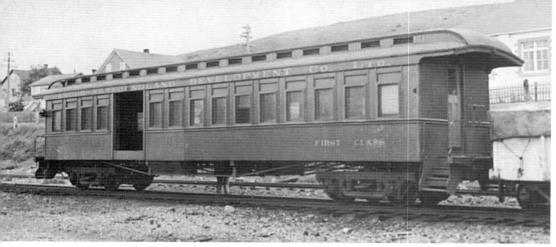

Railway was sold by the AND Co. and became a common carrier, the Grand Falls Central Railway Company, operating only when the ocean port of Botwood was free of ice.

Bowater's Newfoundland Pulp & Paper Company, whose interests are concentrated around the large pulp and paper mill at Corner Brook, had a small railway operation around the mill, connecting with TerraTransport. At one time, the mill was served by two 0-4-0T type locomotives, officially named "Leapin' Lena" and "Sizzlin' Sal". Later they were replaced by a small diesel engine. The steam locomotives also served a logging railway, which was the sometime property of Bowater's, and which extended approximately 20 miles from Deer Lake to Adie's Lake.

The above-mentioned railways discontinued operations with the elimination by TerraTransport of its railway facilities in the Province of Newfoundland in 1988.

Utility rather than grace distinguished 2-4-2T No. 1 of the Buchans Mining Company, built in 1928 by the Baldwin Locomotive Works.

The 4-4-0 was a comparative rarity on the railway lines of Newfoundland. Photo shows Botwood Railway No. 8 at Grand Falls in the 1930s.

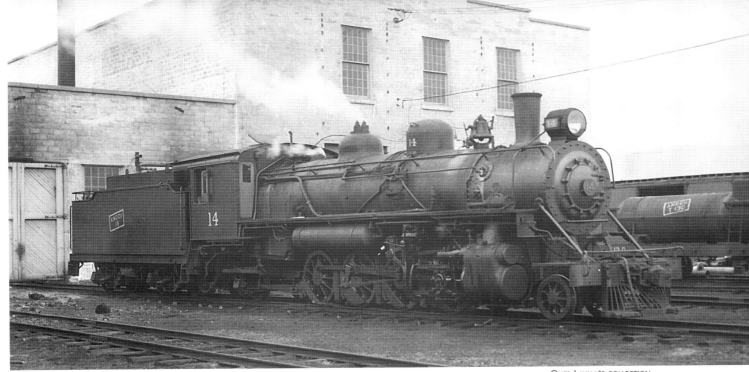

Completely North American lines of Botwood Railway No. 14 belie its origin at the works of the North British Locomotive Company, Glasgow, in 1937. Photo at Botwood in 1952.

Botwood Railway Baldwin 4-6-0 No. 6 at Grand Falls in June 1952.

Grand Falls Central Railway Company

Grand Falls to Bishops Falls, Nfld. .... 12 miles
Bishops Falls to Botwood, Nfld. 10   "
Grand Falls to (CNR) at Windsor, Nfld. 2   "

Gauge: 3 feet, 6 inches.

Chronology:

1957	—Incorporation of Grand Falls Central Railway Company to acquire and operate the "Botwood Railway" of the Anglo-Newfoundland Development Company.
1957, July 1	—Railway taken over and operations commenced.
1988	—Operations discontinued.

Steam Locomotives

No.	Builder	Year	C/N	Type	Cyls.	Dri.	From		To		Notes
1	Baldwin	1907	31075	0-4-0T	12x17"	34"	ANDCo. #1	1957	x 1958		
6	"	1917	45510	4-6-0	17x20"	50"	"	#6	"	"	
9	"	1920	53253	"	"	"	"	#9	"	"	
10	"	"	53503	2-6-2T	15x22"	44"	"	#10	"	"	
12	"	1937	62137	"	16x22"	"	"	#12	"	"	
14	No. Brit.	"	24437	2-8-2	18x24"	48"	"	#14	"	"	
15	"	"	24438	"	"	"	"	#15	"	"	
308	Montreal	1941	69444	"	"	"	CN	#308	"	"	
327	"	1949	76426	"	"	"	"	#327	"	"	
598	Alco	1929	67941	4-6-2	"	52"	"	#598	"	"	
599	"	"	67942	"	"	"	"	#599	"	"	

Internal Combustion Locomotives

No.	Builder	Year	C/N	Type	Weight	H.P.	From		To	Notes
100	Plymouth	1952	5702	- C -			ANDCo. #23	1958		DTC, A
101	GE	1957	33257	B-B	70 ton	720	New			DE
102	"	"	33258	"	"	"	"			"
103	"	"	33259	"	"	"	"			"

Notes: DTC—Diesel Torque Converter.
      DE—Diesel Electric.
      A—No. 23 to Clayton D. Cook Loop Railway in 1987.

ALAN L. THOMAS, COURTESY R. J. SANDUSKY COLLECTION

Newfoundland Hardwoods was the last remaining 3'6"-gauge operation in Newfoundland. This is one of two ex-US Military Plymouth diesels, and is shown switching the Clarenville Creosote Plant in 1967.

Other narrow gauge lines in Newfoundland include the Cassandra Tramway, a two-mile pole-railed tramway extending from Cassandra to Cassandra Brook, opened in 1909; a seven-mile railway, owned by the Newfoundland Iron Ore Company, completed in 1898 from Lower Island Cove to Old Perlican, and abandoned in 1901, and a railway built by the United States Army in 1941 to connect the United States Army Air Force Base at Harmon Field, near Stephenville,

with the Newfoundland Railway at White's Road, a distance of ten miles. This railway was closed in 1963, subsequently taken over by CNR and operated as its Stephenville Branch.

Bell Island, in Conception Bay, was the site of a six-mile 24-inch gauge cable railway built by the Dominion Iron & Steel Co. in 1901, and of the Bell Island Transportation Company, a half-mile cable-operated incline railway which extended from the Ferry Wharf to Upper Bell Island, and carried passengers.

At Clarenville is a small system serving the creosoting plant of Newfoundland Hardwoods. It remains today as the last meaningful rail operation on the island.

LATE ROBERT R. BROWN

A lesser-known Newfoundland "common carrier" was the half-mile long Bell Island Transportation Company, a cable incline which extended from the Ferry Wharf to Upper Bell Island.

LATE ROBERT R. BROWN

11

Alberta Lines

North Western Coal & Navigation Co. Ltd.

Alberta Railway & Coal Company

St. Mary's River Railway Company

Great Falls & Canada Railway Company (USA)

WITH THE OPENING OF THE FIRST SECtions of the Newfoundland systems in 1882, the inauguration of new railway lines having the 3'6" gauge may now be considered to have reached their peak. With narrow gauge systems now functioning in Ontario, Quebec, New Brunswick, Nova Scotia, Prince Edward Island and Newfoundland, it is significant that all except one (the Glasgow and Cape Breton system) used the so-called "British Metric" gauge of 42".

Not so in western Canada. Here, development of small gauge lines took place in the chosen medium of our United States friends, the three-foot gauge. This is not surprising in view of the proximity of the Colorado Rocky Mountain systems which, by the mid-1880s, were approaching their prime and which faced geographic and climatic conditions similar to those prevailing in the Canadian Rockies. The few photographs which we have to illustrate operations on the Alberta systems, the Kaslo and Slocan and the Trail Creek Tramway, will undoubtedly appeal to those who have a predilection for the type of railroading exemplified by the Colorado companies.

While the Canadian Pacific Railway was under construction across the prairies from the Red River to

OMER LAVALLÉE COLLECTION

Diminutive size of North West Coal's Baldwin-built 2-6-0 No. 1 is clearly shown in this picture taken at Dunmore, Alberta in 1890. Canadian Pacific main transcontinental line was to the right of the station.

the Rocky Mountains, public attention was focussed on development of this wide and arid region. The mineral possibilities were known to some extent, particularly coal, which had been first mined and sold to freight teams as early as 1870, from a mine site on the banks of the Oldman River below the present city of Lethbridge. This community, located under the present CPR viaduct, was known as Coalbanks.

Nothing approaching volume production could be achieved without some type of bulk transportation, however, and the operations remained dormant until the Canadian Pacific Railway undertook construction of its transcontinental main line westward from Winnipeg in 1882. At this time, Sir Alexander Galt became interested in development of the Oldman River deposits and on April 25th 1882, incorporated the North Western Coal & Navigation Company in Great Britain, to develop coal deposits in the South Saskatchewan River basin and transport the mineral by steamers along the River and its tributaries.

Canadian Pacific reached Medicine Hat in 1883, and in the autumn of that year, the North West Company initiated work on its project by building the hull of the steamer *"Baroness"* at Coalbanks. Completed in the spring of 1884, the hull was floated down river to Medicine Hat where the machinery was installed and the superstructure built.

Simultaneously, another steamer, the *"Alberta"* and a number of coal barges were constructed at Medicine Hat. The flotilla was completed by a third and smaller vessel, *"Minnow"*, which was purchased at Winnipeg and brought to Medicine Hat by railway.

When the spring runoff raised the river in April 1884, the three steamers made their first trips to Coalbanks. They carried provisions upstream and

St. Mary's River Railway

Commencing Wednesday, November 28th, 1900, trains will run as follows :

GOING SOUTH.				GOING NORTH.
Monday, Wednesday and Friday.				Monday, Wednesday and Friday.
8.00 a.m.	lv	.. Lethbridge ..	ar	4.50 p.m.
9.20 "	"	....Stirling ...	"	3.30 "
10.00 "	"	... Brandley...	"	2.50 "
10.55 "	"	... Magrath ...	"	2.10 "
12.05 p.m.	ar	Spring Coulee	lv	1.15 p.m.

The first timetable of the St. Mary's River line was a small green 2½" x 3¼" card.

propelled loaded coal barges downstream. Though service was offered throughout the 1884 season, it was soon found that the coal barges could only be operated satisfactorily at periods of high water. Even under the most favourable water conditions, the

A construction train of the Alberta Railway & Coal Company photographed on October 1st 1890— the day the line from Lethbridge to Coutts, Alberta was completed.

For the first trip over the St. Mary's River Railway on November 28th 1900, two coaches were borrowed from the Great Falls & Canada Railway. The photo shows P. L. Naismith (centre of the group), the President of the railway, accompanied by railway officers and municipal dignitaries of the town of Magrath, Alberta on this special occasion.

steamers were not sufficiently powerful to propel the barges upstream due to the heavy flow of water and the company terminated the service at the close of 1884 navigation with a determination to replace it with a narrow gauge railway extending from a connection with the Canadian Pacific at Dunmore, a few miles east of Medicine Hat, to Coalbanks.

Authorized by Canadian legislation in 1884, the 109-mile railway was located, surveyed and built within the space of one season. Its location was approved in March 1885, construction was completed by September 1st of that year, and after inspection, the line was officially opened on October 19th 1885. During the same year, a townsite was laid out on the prairie level 300 feet above the river, and named Lethbridge after the president of the North Western company, William Lethbridge. Coal was lifted from the mines at Coalbanks on the river bottoms to the railway terminus at Lethbridge by means of an inclined plane.

The North Western Company's railway, built to a gauge of 36 inches, ran through the present commu-nities of Bow Island, Purple Springs and Taber; it was laid with 28-pound steel rails, and equipped with six Baldwin 2-6-0s and 135 wooden hopper cars. Despite its nickname, "the Turkey Trail", it became one of Canadian Pacific's first prairie feeders and was hauling the respectable figure of 90,000 tons of coal annually by the end of the decade.

On December 31st 1889, another company, the Alberta Railway & Coal Company (which had been incorporated in 1884) leased the North-Western Coal & Navigation Company's lines, with an option to purchase before December 31st 1891. During 1890, the AR&C Co. built a three-foot gauge extension of the original line from Ghent, just east of Lethbridge, to Coutts, on the International Boundary. This line, 64.6 miles long, was completed on October 1st 1890 and was opened to traffic on December 8th of that year. Concurrently, a United States subsidiary of this road was completed from Sweetgrass, Montana, (opposite Coutts) to Great Falls, and a connection with the Great Northern Railway Company. This line was known as the Great Falls & Canada Railway

A work train of the North Western Coal & Navigation Co. is pictured at a loading facility at Lethbridge, Alberta c1885.

Cars of the North Western Coal & Navigation Co. at a coal loading platform c1885. Note the mine cars of coal on the trestle.

An engine house and water tank of the North Western Coal & Navigation Co. appear in this 1885 photograph, probably taken near Lethbridge.

Company, and its rolling stock was used interchangeably with its Canadian counterpart.

In February 1891, the Alberta Railway & Coal Company exercised its option and purchased the Dunmore–Lethbridge line, but operated it for less than three years. On November 27th 1893, this section was leased to Canadian Pacific Railway, and the gauge changed to 4'8½". The CPR used this as the first stage of the railway which was subsequently completed over Crows' Nest Pass into southern British Columbia.

During the 1890s, considerable settlement of the area southwest of Lethbridge took place, largely by Mormons from Utah. (Cardston, Alberta, is named after Charles Ora Card, one of the Mormon leaders). Their efforts to introduce irrigation into the area were partially successful at this early date, and it was largely as a developmental project that the St. Mary's River Railway Company was incorporated in 1900, as a subsidiary of the Alberta Railway & Coal Company. This new company opened a three-foot gauge branch from Stirling to Spring Coulee, Alberta, on November 28th 1900. It was extended to Cardston, with a branch from Raley to Kimball, in 1904. The St. Mary's River Railway apparently did not possess any rolling stock of its own, all of it being supplied by the parent Alberta Railway & Coal Company.

The narrow gauge network continued to have its operating headquarters in Lethbridge, where the double gauge yard was shared with Canadian Pacific trains. As early as 1902, the Alberta company decided to standard gauge the operations of its international line and in September of that year, a third rail for standard gauge equipment was laid from Montana Junction to Stirling, then along the St. Mary's River line as far as Raymond. On January 1st 1903, the AR&C/GF&C main line between Stirling and Great Falls via Coutts/Sweetgrass was converted to standard gauge. A corporate change came about in 1904 when the Alberta company and its subsidiary, the St. Mary's River Railway, were absorbed into a new entity, the Alberta Railway & Irrigation Company. At the same time, the Great Falls & Canada was purchased by the Great Northern Railway.

Authorities differ as to the date on which the line extending from Raymond to Cardston and Kimball was converted to standard gauge, and narrow gauge third rail lifted between Lethbridge and Raymond. It appears probable that the conversion, though planned as early as 1906, did not take place until 1912 when the Irrigation Company was leased to Canadian Pacific in perpetuity.

With the contraction of the narrow gauge network by the mid-1900s, at least two of the 2-6-0 locomotives were moved to the Kicking Horse Pass where they worked on a 36-inch gauge contractor's railway hauling spoil during the construction of Canadian Pacific's spiral tunnels, which were completed in September 1909. One of these engines was abandoned at the site and its stripped remains exist although its fate remains to be decided.

Another engine, No. 16, was presented to the City of Lethbridge for preservation in a park in 1912, but the project was not successful and the locomotive was scrapped in 1916.

One of Alberta Railway & Coal Company's consolidation types forms the background for a group of employees and onlookers at Great Falls, Montana roundhouse in 1895.

Alberta Railway & Coal Company • North Western Coal & Navigation Company
St. Mary's River Railway Company • Great Falls & Canada Railway Company

Dunmore to Lethbridge, NWT (Alta) .... 108.4 miles @ CP		Raley to Kimball, NWT (Alta) .... 12.9 miles **
Montana Jct. (Ghent) to Coutts, NWT (Alta)* .... 64.7 " @ CP		Sweetgrass, Mont.* to Great Falls, Mont. .... 137.0 " @ BN
Stirling to Cardston, NWT (Alta) .... 47.3 " @ CP		

Steam Locomotives

Probably nowhere else in Canada has a motive power roster of a compact railway operation been so elusive as that of the NWC&N Co. and its successor, the AR&C Co. While much of the original data has been documented in builders' records, the subsequent history of the engines (both renumberings and sales) has defied positive identification since apparently no company records were preserved or at least none have come to light. Photographic and other research has partly filled this void, and the findings are so documented in the hope that research might continue.

North Western Coal & Navigation Company

No.	Builder	Year	C/N	Type	Cyls.	Dri.	From	Source	Notes
1	Baldwin	1885	7555	2-6-0	12x16"	37"	New	I	M
2	"	"	7560	"	"	"	"	I	M
3	"	"	7561	"	"	"	"	I	M
4	"	"	7697	"	"	"	"	I	M
5	"	"	7706	"	"	"	"	I	M
6	"	"	7717	"	"	"	"	I	M
7				2-6-0 or 2-4-2T				IV	
8	Baldwin			4-4-0				III	
-	Hinkley	1888	1780	0-6-0			New	I	M
-	"	"	1781	"			"	I	M

Alberta Railway & Coal Company

No.	Builder	Year	C/N	Type	Cyls.	Dri.	From	Source	Notes
1	Baldwin	5/1890	10882	0-6-0	14x18"	37"	New	II	A
2	"	6/1890	11005	2-8-0	16x20"	"	"	II	B
3	"	"	11022	"	"	"	"	II	C
4	"	7/1890	11069	"	"	"	"	II	D
5	"	"	11073	"	"	"	"	II	E
6	"	"	11074	"	"	"	"	II	D
7	"	"	11075	"	"	"	"	II	F
8	"	"	11076	"	"	"	"	II	E
9								IV	
10				2-6-0				IV	
11	Baldwin	5/1890	10847	"	14x18"	41"	New	I	G, M
12	"	"	10880	"	"	"	"	I	G, M
13	"	"	10881	"	"	"	"	II	M
14	"	"	10888	"	"	"	"	II	M
15	Canadian	8/1890	391	"	12x16"	37"	"	II	M
16	"	"	392	"	"	"	"	II	H
17	Baldwin			2-8-0				III	

Sources:
I—Builders' records and selected photographs.
II—Builders' records only.
III—Photographs only.
IV—Other Sources.

Notes:
A—To GF&C, 1901.
B—To Belcher Mountain Ry.
C—To GF&C #3; late 1890s to UC; RGW #01 (1898); RGW #1 (SG-1901); D&RG #554 (1908); D&RG #300.
D—To Puget Sound Mills & Timber Co. in 1901 (#4) and Oct. 1911 (#6).
E—One or both to GF&C; to UC; to D&RGW #554 and #555?.
F—To Eureka & Palisade Ry. #10; Sumpter Valley 2nd or 3rd #15.
G—#11 or #12 to Tanana Valley Ry. (Alaska) #52, 1907.
H—#16 donated to City of Lethbridge 1912; placed in Exhibition Grounds; neglected; sent to Ogden Shops and scrapped by CP in 1916.
M—The Moguls:
(1) • In addition to the roster listings:
  • Two other photographs exist of NWC&N/AR&C engines. Both appear to be of NWC&N 1-6 series 2-6-0s:
  • Two views of engine lettered "AR&C Co." and stated to be "No. 13".
  • A view of engine clearly numbered "15" with straight top boiler, used on narrow gauge railway on construction of CP spiral tunnels in 1908-09.
  • Also existing are the remains of another 2-6-0 (known to be serial 7717 from the salvaged builders' plate) used in this same construction service, with wagon top boiler (as shown in photo as NWC&N Co. #6). It was left derelict on the Yoho Mine spur at base of Mount Stephen on Field Hill in British Columbia and is still extant, although stripped.
(2) —AR&C Co. #13, #14 are reported sold in 1894. #15 may have been sold about same time. In this event, three of the NWC&N Co. 2-6-0s could have been retained and renumbered AR&C Co. 2/#13, 2/#14, 2/#15, as borne out by photographs.
(3) —NWC&N Co. #6 (on Field Hill) had wagon top boiler with bell ahead of two domes; all other photos of NWC&N Co. #1-5 series show parallel boilers with bell behind two domes.
(4) —In relating to rosters of the 2-6-0s on the K&S and TCT, the following appears possible:
  K&S —Two Baldwins; K&S #2 is similar to NWC&N Co. #6.
  TCT —Two Hinkleys (probably converted to 2-6-0s) as TCT #1 and #2.
  —Two 2-6-0s as TCT #4 and #5; one may have been AR&C Co. #15 (Canadian).

St. Mary's River Railway Company

There is no record of motive power owned by this company; it is thought to have been provided by the AR&C Co.

Great Falls & Canada Railway Company

Rosters refer to locomotives lettered for this company, but details not known. It is possible that individual AR&C Co. locomotives were lettered for the GF&C but remained in AR&C Co. road number series.

---

*Coutts and Sweetgrass have a common station at the International Boundary.
**See the note following Chronology.

Gauge: 3 feet, 0 inches.

Chronology:

1882, Apr. 25	—Incorporation of North Western Coal & Navigation Company in Great Britain. Company was incorporated in Canada in 1884.
1884	—Incorporation of Alberta Railway & Coal Company.
1885, Apr. 1	—NWC&N Co. opens railway from Dunmore Junction to Coalbanks (Lethbridge).
1887, Oct. 2	—Great Falls & Canada Railway Company incorporated in the US as a subsidiary of the Alberta Railway & Coal Company.
1889, Dec. 31	—NWC&N Co. leased to AR&C Co. with option to purchase before December 31st 1891.
1890, Apr. 1	—GF&C Ry. opened for service Sweetgrass to Shelby, Mont.
1890, Oct. 1	—AR&C Co. completes line from Montana Junction to Coutts and connection with GF&C Ry.
1890, Dec. 8	—AR&C Co. Montana Junction-Coutts line opened for service, and GF&C Ry. line opened Shelby to Great Falls. Through rail connection established this date between Lethbridge and Great Falls.
1891, Feb.	—AR&C Co. exercises option purchasing NWC&N Co. with transaction retroactive to December 31st 1889.
1893, Nov. 27	—Lethbridge to Dunmore Junction section leased to Canadian Pacific Railway Company. Subsequently, gauge between Montana Junction and Dunmore Junction changed from 3'0" to 4'8½". Third rail for standard gauge trains laid between Montana Junction and Lethbridge.
1897, Dec. 31	—Lethbridge–Dunmore section sold outright to Canadian Pacific Railway Company. AR&C Co. retains running rights into Lethbridge on double-gauge section from Montana Junction.
1900	—Incorporation of St. Mary's River Railway Company, a "paper" subsidiary of Alberta Railway & Coal Company.
1900, Nov. 28	—StMR Ry. Co. opened for traffic Stirling-Spring Coulee.
1901, Aug. 1	—AR&C Co. sells GF&C Ry. to Montana Great Northern Railway Company, a subsidiary of Great Northern Railway Company.
1902, Mar. 10	—Preparation begun for standard gauging of GF&C Ry. between Sweetgrass and Great Falls. Work completed late in 1902.
1902	—AR&C Co. begins preparation for standard-gauging line between Montana Junction and Coutts.
1903, Jan. 1	—Inauguration of standard gauge operation between Lethbridge and Great Falls, over AR&C Co. and GF&C Ry. (MGN Ry.). Third rail retained for StMR Ry. Co. trains between Stirling, Montana Junction and Lethbridge.
1903, Jan. 4	—GF&C Ry. Co. sold by Montana Great Northern Ry. Co. to its parent, Great Northern Railway Co.
1903	—St. Mary's River Ry. Co. extends narrow gauge line from Spring Coulee to Cardston and builds branch from Raley to Kimball.

This picture is captioned "First locomotive into Lethbridge" and shows one of North Western Coal & Navigation Company's Baldwin 2-6-0s.

NORTH WESTERN COAL & NAVIGATION CO. LTD. 2-8-0
Baldwin Locomotive Works, 1885

Road Nos. 6	Date .... Nov. 1885
Gauge .... 36"	Cylinders .... 12"x26"
Type 2-6-0	(diam. & stroke)
Builder .... BLW	Driving Wheels .... 37"

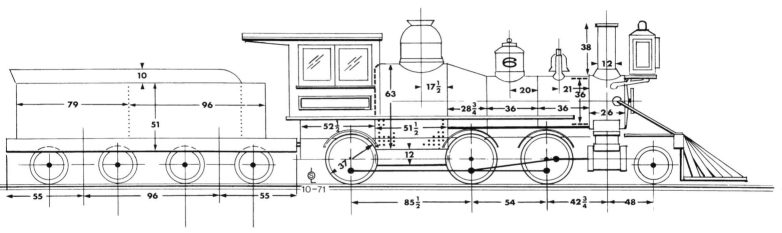

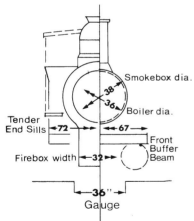

1904, June —Alberta Railway & Irrigation Company formed from combined Alberta Railway & Coal Company, St. Mary's River Railway Company and Canadian North West Irrigation Company.

1912 —Former StMR Ry. Co. line between Stirling and Cardston converted from 3'0" to 4'8½" gauge, and Raley-Kimball branch abandoned. ** Third rail for narrow gauge between Stirling, Montana Junction and Lethbridge also lifted at this time.

1912, Jan. 1 —AR&I Co. leased to Canadian Pacific Railway Company for 999 years. Operation of railway by CPR assumed June 2nd 1912.

**Kimball branch roadbed retained and about 8 miles of it built upon again by CPR in constructing Woolford Subdivision, from Raley to Whisky Gap in 1929.

At least two of the Alberta Railway & Coal Company's 2-6-0s rounded out their careers working trains of excavated spoil during the construction of Canadian Pacific's Spiral Tunnels in the Kicking Horse valley east of Field, British Columbia in 1907 and 1908. This photograph shows one of them, No. 15, with level top boiler and bell next to cab, at the interchange with the standard gauge Canadian Pacific main line near the base of Mount Stephen at that time. The remains of a second 2-6-0, identified as original No. 6 of the North Western Coal & Navigation Company, can still be seen in the same area as this photograph was taken.

•12•
Lake Temiscamingue Colonization Railway Company

APART FROM THE 36-INCH GAUGE RAILWAY at Sydney, Nova Scotia opened in 1870, the only other railways of this narrow width to be constructed in eastern Canada were built in the Province of Quebec by the colonization societies, supported by the Roman Catholic Church, which were formed in the 1880s to further the settling and agricultural development of the fertile hinterland along the north shores of the St. Lawrence and Ottawa rivers.

One of the first areas to receive attention from colonization groups was that of the region of Lake Temiscamingue, on the Ontario-Quebec border, on the upper Ottawa River. With the extension of the Canada Central Railway toward North Bay, as the initial link in the transcontinental railway in the early 1880s, rail transportation was brought almost to the "front door" of the Temiscamingue area at Mattawa, where the railway turns away westward from the Ottawa River. However, forty miles of the Ottawa separated Mattawa from the area of settlement, forty miles which formed one of the most turbulent stretches of this river, dropping some 54 feet from the foot of Lake Temiscamingue to the site of Mattawa.

One of the earliest proposals to make this route navigable was advanced by an Oblate priest, Father Paradis, who envisioned the building of a dam across the Ottawa at Mattawa, raising the level of the river by 32 feet, and removing the shoals at the head of Long Sault, which in turn, would have the effect of lowering the level of Lake Temiscamingue by some 22 feet. Thereby, the Long Sault and other rapids would be submerged, and an uninterrupted navigation of 115 miles achieved above Mattawa. The lowering of the lake level would also release thousands of acres of fertile land along its shores for cultivation.

On December 12th 1884, la Société de Colonisation du Lac Témiscamingue (the Temiscamingue Colonization Society) was formed, and its President was another Oblate, Father P. E. Gendreau. The Society abandoned the Paradis project, because of its cost, and went to the Federal Government for aid to

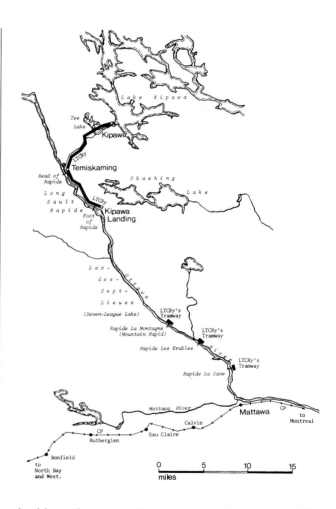

build a railway six miles long around the most difficult rapid at Long Sault, and to build light tramways around the three other rapids in the 32-mile route between Mattawa and Long Sault, the La Cave, Les Erables and La Montagne rapids. Federal and Provincial subsidies were eventually forthcoming to aid this project, and on July 20th 1886, by Order of the Privy Council, the Lake Temiscamingue Colonization Railway Company was formed to build a steam-operated 3-foot gauge line around the Long Sault portage, and light tramway lines for horse haulage, probably of the same gauge, around the three lesser rapids. A year sufficed to construct this system, and it was opened to service on June 9th 1887. During the summer of

This is the only known photograph taken on the Lake Temiscamingue Colonization Railway. It shows H. K. Porter 0-4-2T locomotive, road number unknown, in service near Temiscamingue, Quebec. The builder's record, incidentally, lists this engine as 2-4-0T.

1888, the Long Sault section was extended overland an additional nine miles to Lake Kipawa, reaching its full extent of 15.2 miles. In connection with the railway, a steamer service was opened in the same year on Lake Temiscamingue, and a tug and barge service in the four other gaps between the rapids.

In January 1891, Canadian Pacific Railway offered to take over the line and build a new standard gauge line all the way from Mattawa to Lake Kipawa. While this undertaking was accepted, it did not come about until the close of navigation in 1893, at which time the narrow gauge was abandoned.

Lake Temiscamingue Colonization Railway Company

Long Sault of the Ottawa River to Lake Kipawa, Que. .... 15.2 miles
(also light tramway lines around Ottawa River portages)

Gauge: 3 feet, 0 inches.

Chronology:

1886, July 20 —Incorporation of Lake Temis-camingue Colonization Railway Company.

1887, June 9 —Opened for traffic Long Sault to Kipawa.

1893 —Line abandoned and right-of-way purchased by Canadian Pacific Railway Company who constructed standard gauge on it as part of new branch from Mattawa to Kipawa.

Steam Locomotives

No.	Builder	Year	C/N	Type	Cyls.	Dri.	From	To	Notes
	Porter	1886	756	0-4-2T	6x10"		New	MCR ?	A

Notes: A—Porter records say this locomotive was 2-4-0 but photo shows it as 0-4-2T. Line also said to have possessed a 2-8-0 and both engines, with rolling stock, thought to have been sold to Montfort Colonization Railway Company which was built in same year as LTCR abandoned.

•13•
Montfort Colonization Railway

No photographs have come to light illustrating the equipment or the operations of the Montfort Colonization Railway in its narrow gauge days. Robert Sandusky has prepared this artistic impression showing a Montfort train, at left, meeting the Canadian Pacific Laurentian main line train at old Montfort Junction, a few miles north of Shawbridge, Quebec in the mid-1890s. The narrow gauge line curved left, in the background, crossing the Rivière du Nord, then ascending a grade westward to the community of Morin Flats, Quebec.

WE CAN ONLY SURMISE THAT WHEN THE Lake Temiscamingue Colonization Railway was finally torn up in 1893-94, its salvageable assets, possibly including the rail, and the locomotives and rolling stock, may have gone to the Montfort Colonization Railway, which was incorporated under the statutes of Quebec in 1890, and in 1893 commenced construction of a three-foot gauge railway into the valley of Montfort in the Laurentian mountains to the north of Montreal.

The Catholic Church was also interested in settling this area, and in any reference to colonization in Quebec, mention should always be made of Rev. Father F. X. A. Labelle (died 1891), the energetic parish priest of St. Jerome, Quebec, who founded sixty villages between 1869 and 1891, who was one of the principal advocates of the Northern Colonization Railway (opened Montreal-St. Jerome in 1876), was Provincial Deputy Minister of Agriculture and Colonization in 1888, and was elevated to the episcopacy in 1889. "Curé Labelle" was a large man, physically, weighing over 300 pounds, and by reason of his accomplishments, he has become a legendary figure in an area which is today the backyard summer and

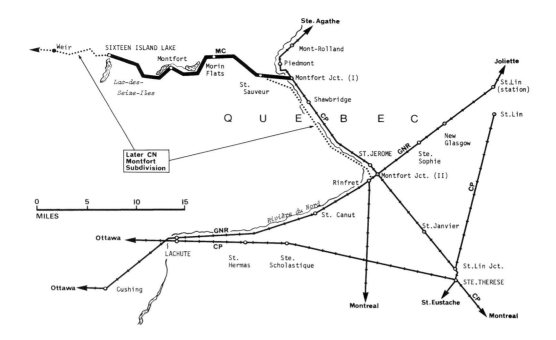

winter playground of Montreal.

But in the 1890s development was still going on, and in connection with the construction of the Canadian Pacific Railway northward toward Ste-Agathe and St-Jovite, the Montfort Colonization Society started its railway at Montfort Junction. This was the first of two such places to bear that name and was located at what later became Vimy siding on Canadian Pacific's Ste-Agathe Subdivision. There, over 70 years later, could still be discerned the roadbed of the little three-foot gauge carrier which crossed the valley floor, then, by means of two rather prodigious grades of 168 feet per mile (3.2%) climbed first into the basin of Morin Heights (then called Morin Flats) and St-Sauveur-des-Monts, then up to Lac St. Francois-Xavier at Montfort, Quebec.

The railway was completed to the foot of the second grade, at Lac Chevreuil, in 1893, and in the following year it was extended up to Montfort and over the hill to Sixteen Island Lake (Lac des Seize Iles), just 21 miles from Montfort Junction.

(Care should be taken not to confuse the two Montfort Junctions. The second Montfort Junction was at the point just south of St-Jerome where the Great Northern Railway of Canada crossed the Canadian Pacific Ste-Agathe Subdivision).

Trains commenced operation on the initial 10-mile section in June 1894, and by the end of the year were running through to Sixteen Island Lake. In the ensuing four years, traffic increased appreciably, the principal cargo being lumber, and in 1897, it was decided to widen the gauge to standard width, and extend the railway farther westward toward Arundel and Huberdeau. This was a logical step, as the railway was a feeder to the Canadian Pacific Railway.

The subsequent history of the Montfort Colonization Railway as a standard gauge line does not concern us here, except that the change of gauge was effected some time before June 30th 1898. Suffice it to say that the lower two or three miles were subsequently abandoned, after the railway was purchased by the Great Northern Railway of Canada in February 1903. The remainder continued to operate, through inheritance, by Canadian National Railways until June 1962, when it was abandoned. The grading and alignment of the original narrow gauge line were preserved almost exactly up to the end, even to the 3%-plus grade at Lac Chevreuil, which remained a silent monument to the end of Canadian narrow gauge railways of the 36-inch persuasion.

Montfort Colonization Railway Company

Montfort Junction to Sixteen-Island Lake, Que. .... 21.0 miles   aban.

Gauge: 3 feet, 0 inches.

Chronology:

1890	—Incorporation of the Montfort Colonization Railway Company.
1893	—Construction commenced at Montfort Junction (with Canadian Pacific near Vimy siding north of Shawbridge, Que.), and completed as far as Lac Chevreuil, Que., 10.0 miles.
1894	—Railway opened for service; extended a further 11 miles to Sixteen-Island Lake.

Steam Locomotives

Details unknown, but thought to have been the two (?) locomotives from the Lake Témiscamingue Colonization Railway Company (q.v.) which was abandoned at the time that the Montfort Railway was constructed and both railways were projects of colonization societies supported by the Roman Catholic Church.

1898	—During year ending June 30th 1898, gauge changed to 4'8½". Name changed to Montfort & Gatineau Colonization Railway Company.
1903, Feb. 10	—M&GC Ry. Co. sold to the Great Northern Railway of Canada, later forming part of Canadian Northern Railway system and, after 1918, Canadian National Railways.

•14•
Kaslo & Slocan Railway Company

WE MUST RETURN TO THE WEST ONCE again, to examine the next 36-inch gauge railway to be built. This line, the Kaslo & Slocan Railway Company, was chartered on April 23rd 1892, to build from Kaslo on Kootenay Lake, up the valley of the Kaslo River to Sandon, British Columbia, a mining town which had got its start in the same month as the railway was incorporated. Sandon was the centre of a mineral boom in silver-lead ore, and it was located high in the inaccessible mountain range between Slocan and Kootenay lakes.

The railway was the project of the Great Northern Railway, and was built as part of that company's in-filtration into southern British Columbia—in this

particular case, as an adjunct of a route which had been completed from Bonners Ferry, Idaho, to the foot of Kootenay Lake, and of a steamer line on the lake, which connected this standard gauge link with the town of Kaslo. Completion of the three-foot carrier would enable Sandon ore to be taken to Kaslo, then shipped down the lake to the railway connection with the United States at Kuskanook, BC.

Starting at Kaslo, the alignment was a precipitous one. The railway required a switchback just to get out of, and above, the town, then it twisted back and forth following the turns of the Kaslo River for some 20 miles, to Zincton. Here, at the watershed between Kootenay and Slocan lakes, the railway stayed more

A Kaslo & Slocan Railway train posed for this photograph at an unidentified British Columbia location in the mid-1890s.

Kaslo & Slocan mixed train at Whitewater, British Columbia in 1898. Consist of the Kaslo-bound train comprises three ore box cars, combination car No. 4 and coach No. 3.

or less at the summit level, but clung to the ledges of the mountain side, finally curving around the Payne Bluff, into Sandon. It was completed and opened for service on November 20th 1895, for a distance of 29 miles.

Initially, the railway prospered, and the vein of ore found at its upper terminal turned out to be one of the richest ever found in the Slocan district; shipments in the first years averaged 239 ounces of silver, and 47½% of lead, per ton of concentrate.

On January 1st 1899, the Kaslo & Slocan was taken over by a new company, the Kootenay Railway & Navigation Company, which had been incorporated in London on August 8th 1898, but the Great

Kaslo & Slocan's No. 3 was an outside-framed consolidation of uncertain origin.

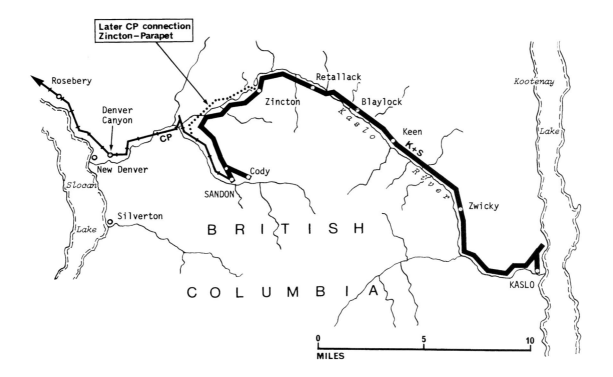

Later CP connection
Zincton–Parapet

Rosebery

Denver Canyon

New Denver

Slocan

Lake

Silverton

CP

SANDON

Cody

Zincton

Retallack

Blaylock

Keen

K+S

Zwicky

KASLO

Kaslo River

Kootenay Lake

B R I T I S H

C O L U M B I A

0   5   10

MILES

Northern retained its controlling interest. The KR&N Company also operated the steamer route, and the standard gauge railway at the foot of the lake.

In 1900, the town of Sandon was destroyed by fire, and though it was rebuilt, prosperity had started on the decline, and the railway proved to be an expensive one to maintain, especially the many wooden trestles and bridges, and the winding route of the 45-pound steel rails.

In 1908 and again in 1909, the railway was dealt a stunning blow by landslides, which took out the track in many places, and forced suspension of service between McGuigan and Sandon. While the Great Northern was debating whether to rebuild or to abandon the line, the final blow came in July 1910 when a tremendous forest fire burned most of the remaining buildings and bridges, the heat so twisting the rails that further operations were rendered hopeless.

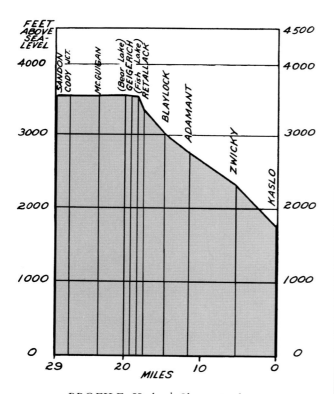

PROFILE: *Kaslo & Slocan Railway*

A "kink" in bridge No. 26, after it was hit by a snowslide.

Baldwin 2-6-0 No. 2 at Kaslo, British Columbia in 1898. This locomotive is one of two said to have come to the K&S from one of the Alberta lines.

When the Great Northern Railway declined to rebuild the railway, a group of Kaslo people purchased the railway on May 27th 1911 for $25,000, and after working on it for the summer, were able to reopen it for limited service between Kaslo and Sproule, 15 miles, by September 15th. In April 1912, they consented to an arrangement whereby the Canadian Pacific would take it over and standard gauge it, and while some of the narrow gauge equipment was used in the summer of 1912 during the reconstruction between Kaslo and Zincton, that was the last year for the narrow gauge. The section from Zincton to Sandon was abandoned completely, and the railway built down the valley from Zincton to Parapet, whence Canadian Pacific already had a steep (4.9%) standard gauge branch into Sandon.

Now standard gauged, the remaining portion of the former K&S between Kaslo and Zincton continued to be used by the CPR until abandonment in 1956.

Kaslo & Slocan Railway Company

Kaslo to Sandon, BC .... 28.8 miles aban.
Junction to Cody, BC .... 3.0   "   "

Gauge: 3 feet, 0 inches.

Chronology:

1892, Apr. 23 —Incorporation of Kaslo & Slocan Railway Company.
1895, Nov. 20 —Railway completed and opened for service from Kaslo to Sandon.
1897 —Branch completed from Junction to Cody.
1898, Aug. 8 —Incorporation of the Kootenay Railway & Navigation Company in Great Britain to operate the Kaslo & Slocan Railway, the Bedlington & Nelson Railway and steamer services in Canada, on behalf of the parent company, the Great Northern Railway of the USA.
1909, July —Service discontinued between McGuigan and Sandon, on account of slides.
1910, July —Service completely discontinued following forest fires.

Steam Locomotives

No.	Builder	Year	C/N	Type	Cyls.	Dri.	From	To	Notes
1	Baldwin			2-6-0	16x20"	37"	?	x or sold after 1912	A
2	"			"	"	"	?	"	A
3	"	1888	9795	2-8-0	"	38"	?	"	B
4	K&S	1904		0-4-0				"	C

Notes: A—Probably ex Alberta Ry. & Coal Co. or North Western Coal & Nav. Co. (q.v.). #2 similar to NWC&N Co. #6 in design.

B—Bought second hand by Great Northern Ry. and rebuilt in Spokane shops; had outside frames.

C—#4 was built at Kaslo. It had a vertical boiler and single cylinder.

1911, May 27 —Local syndicate purchases railway and reopens it on Sept. 15th 1911 between Kaslo & Sproule.

1912, April —Railway transferred to British Columbia government; section from Kaslo to Zincton later taken over by Canadian Pacific Railway Co. and standard-gauged in 1912 and 1913.

•15•

Trail Creek Tramway

Columbia & Western Railway Company

SHORTER-LIVED, AND A LITTLE FARTHER south in British Columbia, was the 13-mile, 36-inch gauge railway which carried the gold-copper ores of the Rossland and LeRoi mining region down two switchbacks and 4% + grades by way of the valley of Trail Creek to its discharge into the Columbia River—known variously as the Trail Creek Tramway or the Columbia & Western Railway.

The first claims had been staked at Rossland in 1890, and after mining had begun, the concentrate was shipped down a wagon road to Trail Creek Landing where it was loaded on board Columbia River vessels for transportation to, and processing in, the United States.

In 1895, F. Augustus Heinze, a Montana mining man, formulated a plan to build a smelter at the Landing and bring the ore down from Rossland on a narrow gauge light railway. Construction started early in 1896 on the Trail Creek Tramway and it was opened for traffic between LeRoi and the Landing, by now renamed Trail, on June 1st 1896. In the interim, however, the British Columbia Government had granted Heinze a charter for the Columbia & Western Railway Company, which took over the rights, etc., of the Trail Creek Tramway, but also conferred large powers in respect to the building of railways in southern British Columbia.

It was out of a desire to secure this charter that the Canadian Pacific Railway Company, in 1898, purchased the railway and the smelter from Heinze and his associates, the narrow gauge being converted to standard in 1899 or 1900. The smelter, by the way, developed into the Consolidated Mining & Smelting Company, later Teck Cominco.

W. GIBSON KENNEDY COLLECTION

The first train from Trail to Rossland, British Columbia on the Trail Creek Tramway of the Columbia & Western Railway, June 1st 1896. The train, headed by a 2-6-0 thought to be No. 1, is pictured at Trail, British Columbia.

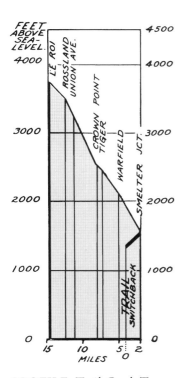

PROFILE: *Trail Creek Tramway*

Much of the narrow gauge equipment was sold to the then-building White Pass & Yukon Route, including a passenger car which was said to have been the private car of Brigham Young, the Mormon leader. Some of the other cars, in spite of their small size, were mounted on standard gauge trucks and used by the Canadian Pacific Railway as second-class cars.

Unidentified Trail Creek Tramway 2-6-0 loaded on board a Canadian Pacific flatcar at Smelter Junction destined for parts unknown.

Trail Creek Tramway (1895)
Columbia & Western Railway Company (1896-1898)

Trail to LeRoi, BC .... 13.6 miles

Gauge: 3 feet, 0 inches.

Chronology:

1895	—Trail Creek Tramway Company organized by F. A. Heinze to build railway from Rossland to Trail Creek Landing, BC.
1896, Apr. 17	—Incorporation of the Columbia & Western Railway Company to take over the charter rights and franchises of Trail Creek Tramway Co.
1896, June 1	—Railway opened for traffic.
1898	—Columbia & Western Railway Company, including Trail Creek Tramway, sold to Canadian Pacific Railway Company.
1899 or 1900	—Gauge changed from 3'0" to 4'8½".

Steam Locomotives

Possibly five locomotives, numbered 1 to 5, all 2-6-0.

The history of these engines is linked to (a) the narrow gauge Alberta lines—NWC&N Co./AR&C Co. and (b) the WP&YR Source data in all instances is conflicting and vague.

Notations in Canadian Pacific stock book show:

    1. Hinkley, 12x18" cylinders, 31" drivers—sold Nov. 1899 to McLean Bros. of Vancouver.

    2. Hinkley, 12x18" cylinders, 31" drivers—sold Oct. 1900 to WP&YR (q.v.) possibly WP&YR #64.

    3. Rogers, 14½x18" cylinders, 36" drivers—sold July 1900 to WP&YR (q.v.) possibly WP&YR #65.

    #4 and #5 are not listed in the stock book, but if they were later acquired, probably they came from NWC&N Co./AR&C Co. through Canadian Pacific.

    Photograph of an unidentified 2-6-0 loaded on a flat car is not a Hinkley. It is possibly #3 (see WP&YR #65).

    Two TCT locomotives are reported "acquired from Lethbridge".

Suppositions: #1, #2 ex NWC&N Co. Hinkleys, converted from 0-6-0.

    #3 may be Brooks, not Rogers. Previous owner unknown.

    #4, #5 possibly ex NWC&N Co./AR&C Co.; one of them could be ex AR&C Co. #15.

•16•
White Pass & Yukon Route

British Columbia Yukon Railway

British Yukon Railway Company

Pacific & Arctic Railway & Navigation Company (USA)

THE THIRD NARROW-GAUGE RAILWAY TO have its birth in the 1890s, like its two predecessors, owes its existence to a mining discovery—one of the most spectacular of all on this continent—the Klondike rush of 1898 in Canada's Yukon Territory. This railway, the White Pass & Yukon Route, is also the only narrow-gauge system left in operation.

A gold strike at Bonanza Creek, in the month of August 1896, set off the "gold fever" in the Yukon River region, that drew thousands upon thousands of speculators into the Territory, reaching a climax in 1898. At this time, at that latitude, no transportation existed inland from the Pacific Coast, and the gold-seekers landed at the little United States port of Skagway, making their way, on foot, over Chilkoot Pass and White Pass.

So great was the demand for transportation that the rush gave impetus to an audacious plan to build a narrow-gauge railway from Skagway, over White Pass, to Bennett in British Columbia, then on into the Yukon. To prosecute this, there were incorporated, in 1897, three separate companies—the Pacific & Arctic Railway & Navigation Company (in the Territory of Alaska), the British Columbia Yukon Railway Company (in the Province of British Columbia) and the British Yukon Mining, Trading & Transportation Company (in Yukon Territory). Together, these three railways would form a continuous rail link from Skagway to Fort Selkirk on the Yukon River, some 325 miles. The line was surveyed in the spring of 1898 by Michael J. Heney, an engineer, who, with the support of two other engineers, Sir Thomas Tancrede of London, and Samuel H. Graves of the United States, located the railway over its most difficult section, the initial portion out of Skagway over White Pass. At the end of May 1898, construction was started, and on July 21st of that year, the first train ever to operate in Alaska hauled excursionists for four miles up the Skagway River.

On July 20th 1898, the charter rights and concessions of the three constituent railways were entrusted to a new holding company, the White Pass & Yukon Railway Company Limited, which was organized in London, England.

Construction reached the summit of White Pass, at 2,885 feet, twenty miles from Skagway, by mid-February 1899, and on July 6th 1899, it reached Bennett, at the head of the lake of the same name. This section included a 250-foot tunnel, the 215-foot-high Dead Horse Gulch viaduct, 3.9% grades and 20° curves. During the summer of 1899, construction was also started southward from Whitehorse, and on July 29th 1900, this section was joined with that from Skagway, at Caribou Crossing (Carcross) at a golden spike ceremony. On August 15th 1900, regular service was started between Skagway and Whitehorse.

In June 1900, a 2½-mile portage railway at Taku was incorporated into the WP&YR, being part of a water route operated by the company in connection with the railway. A subsidiary, British Yukon Navigation Company (BYN), operated steamers on the Yukon River between Whitehorse and Dawson City, 434 miles. Between 1910 and 1918, the railway also operated a branch from MacRae to Pueblo, a copper mine near Whitehorse. In spite of its plan to build north from Whitehorse to Fort Selkirk, that extension was never built.

The WP&YR operated a large fleet of passenger-carrying steamboats in the lakes and rivers of the Yukon, right into central Alaska. It also operated ocean freighters, carrying both bulk and containers, from the 1950s until 1982. It even built a hotel—the Atlin Inn, in 1913—operating it until shutdown in 1936.

The most serious loss of company employees occurred in 1918 as a result of a disaster involving a coastal vessel of the Canadian Pacific Railway. The steamship *"Princess Sophia"* left Skagway on October 23rd for Vancouver. Early on October 24th she struck

Overhanging cliff in Skagway River valley dwarfs miniature 2-8-0 No. 68 of the White Pass & Yukon Route in the 1920s.

US Army 2-8-2 brings train through White Pass & Yukon Route's only tunnel, c1942.

Vanderbilt Reef in the Lynn Canal, midway between Skagway and Juneau. A severe storm prevented rescue efforts from being undertaken, with the result that she was driven across the reef into deep water where she sank. All 343 passengers and crew were lost and among the passengers were 84 employees, a few of them railway employees, but most being homeward-bound workers on the company's now-closed-for-winter shipyard and steamboats.

Of the 110 miles of line operated in 1900, 67½ miles (to Carcross, Yukon) were in operating condition in 2004, although scheduled services ran only as far as mile 40.6 (Bennett, British Columbia). The line retains its 36-inch gauge, and, for the tourists who travel over the line every summer, its "Klondike" atmosphere, engendered by the use of open-platformed parlour cars. The fortunes of the WP&YR continued to be favourable and, in 1979, the Executive Offices were moved from Vancouver to Whitehorse.

Unfortunately for the WP&YR, in 1982 world metal prices fell drastically, resulting in the closure of its only remaining mining freight customer, Cyprus Anvil Mine, the major shipper for which the line and rolling stock had been upgraded in 1969. With the only significant traffic source for the railway gone, regular train operation ceased. Then, in 1988, the decision was made to implement a summer tourist train operation in conjunction with cruise ships calling at the port of Skagway. In that first exclusively-tourist season, only the *Summit Excursions* ran, to the White Pass and return. In 1989, the through-service train to Fraser, British Columbia (then bus to Whitehorse) was added, as well as the Chilkoot Trail Service, using a track car and trailer between Fraser and Bennett. The response was so great that, in 1999, the railway repurchased five diesel-electric locomotives from Sociedad Colombiana de Transporte Ferrovario to whom they had been sold in 1992. These units were all manufactured by Montreal Locomotive Works in 1969.

Before the disastrous days of late 1982, the WP&YR management considered that the reintroduction of a limited steam operation would prove to be an attraction to cruise ship passengers. Accordingly, 2-8-2 type locomotive 73, which had been retired in 1963, and which was on display at Bennett, was refurbished and operated that year. When tourist train operations again started in 1988, the steam excursions also resumed. To provide some back-up for this service, a 2-8-0 type locomotive, No. 40, was leased in 2000. This locomotive, originally operated on the Guatemala railways, had been acquired by a tourist railway in Colorado. No. 40 did not meet WP&YR requirements, resulting in the cancellation of this lease, and the return of the locomotive to Colorado. However, future steam operation seems positive with the railway planning to refurbish another steam locomotive in 2005.

The tourist train operation has been very successful. In 1988 39000 passengers were carried; in 1997, 213000; and a record-breaking 404722 in 2004. Indeed, all of the previously-described tourist trains were scheduled for operation in 2005. In addition, the railway owns three docks at Skagway suitable for the mooring of cruise ships. These not only provide revenue to the company, but also feature direct access to the tourist trains.

The importance of the White Pass & Yukon Route as an outstanding example of the engineering profession was recognized in 1994 when the railway was designated an "International Historic Civil Engineering Landmark" by the American Society of Engineers, a distinction which, to that time in Canada at least, was held only by the Quebec Bridge.

In June 1959, a variety of rolling stock, headed by steam locomotive No. 73, is stopped at Inspiration Point, mile 16.9, where passengers were allowed to disembark, stretch their legs, and admire the view down towards Lynn Canal.

Thunderbird-branded General Electric diesel-electric No. 90, the first "growler" to be acquired by the WP&YR, switches a freight train at Whitehorse, Yukon in June 1959.

The wharf at Skagway, Alaska is the scene of great activity as passengers board a WP&YR train for the journey to Bennett, British Columbia. The date appears to be in the 1920s.

A WP&YR passenger train proceeds c1930 down what was Skagway's main street when the town site was surveyed. Imaginatively named "Broadway", it housed a liquor store and ice cream parlour, both prominent in the foreground, as well as a contemporary automobile.

A mountainous backdrop is the setting for the entry into Broadway of a WP&YR passenger train c1930. The Skagway offices of Canadian National, Canadian Pacific and the Alaska Steamship Company are all prominent in this view.

WP&YR's main line headed up Broadway when this photograph was made in the 1930s. During World War II, the line was moved southeast (two blocks to the left) to follow the foot of the mountain at the city limit.

The fabled "Duchess" and open passenger car 232 on the Atlin tramway. Note that front drivers are not connected; the little engine, now preserved at Carcross, Yukon, is a 2-4-0T, not an 0-6-0T. Canadian Pacific's 1919 photo was taken to promote its tourist steamship between BC and Skagway. In background at right is the BYN sternwheeler "Tutshi".

In 1959, there was no market for scrap metal in Skagway, so the WP&YR yard still contained an interesting selection of rolling stock and derelict motive power, much of which was disposed of within a few years.

An impression of northern altitudes is created by this photograph of a WP&YR southbound passenger train in a cloud-decked mountain landscape beside Lake Bennett, British Columbia.

WP&YR vintage-era parlour cars at Bennett flanked, at left, by the station and dining room, and at the right by the old wooden church which is a familiar landmark. This picture was taken about 1930, but the scene is much the same today.

In June 1959, WP&YR steam locomotive No. 73 hauls a mixed train southbound past Fraser Lake, helped by a mid-train diesel engine located just ahead of the author's passenger car, baggage car No. 207.

Three-way stub switch leads to roundhouse and shops at left, and passenger yard at right, at Skagway, in June 1959.

A mixed train, headed by United States Army 2-8-2 with WP&YR 2-8-0 in middle, crosses Dead Horse Gulch viaduct in Alaska during October 1946.

Those who regard North American narrow gauge in a historical context should examine this illustration closely. Every man-made object in it—the 1200-hp diesel engines, the concentrate containers, the (second) Dead Horse Gulch bridge, even the new White Pass Tunnel from which the train is emerging—has been put into use since 1968.

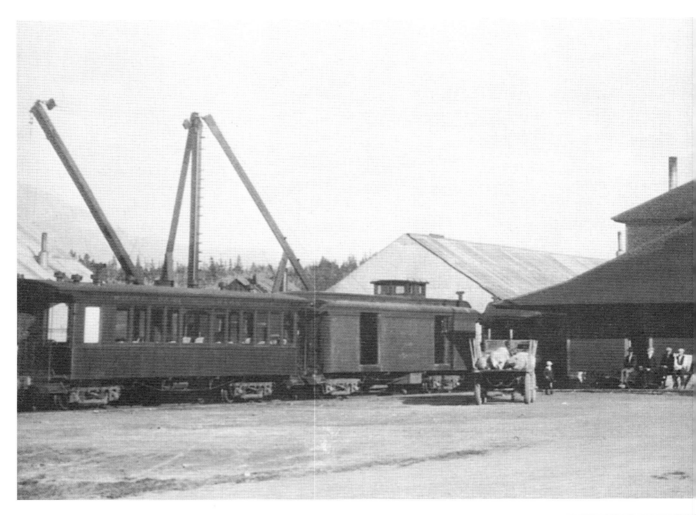

Newly-painted Baldwin 2-8-2 No. 73 backs on to the southbound train at Bennett, British Columbia for the run over the White Pass to Skagway, Alaska in June 1959.

The WP&YR station at Whitehorse, Yukon in the late 1920s or early 1930s. Note the arch-roofed parlour car in the train consist in front of the station at left.

View in White Pass & Yukon Route's Skagway yard, in June 1959.

White Pass & Yukon Route

"Second generation" on the White Pass. No. 101, the first Alco-MLW 1200-hp unit, equipped with wedge plow and ready for Yukon winter, at Whitehorse.

Omer Lavallée

Coal stove in corner contrasts strongly with tubular-framed, upholstered parlour car chairs inside car 240, at Skagway in 1959.

White Pass & Yukon Route

Pacific & Arctic Railway & Navigation Company
British Columbia-Yukon Railway Company

British Yukon Railway Company

Skagway to International Boundary, White Pass	20.4 miles	@	
International Boundary to Yukon-BC Boundary	32.2 "	@	
Taku Tramway, Atlin Lake to Taku Arm, BC	2.5 "	aban.	
Yukon-BC Boundary to Whitehorse, YT	58.1 "	@	
Macrae to Pueblo, YT	10.8 "	aban.	

Gauge: 3 feet, 0 inches.

Chronology:

1897, Jan. —Incorporation of the Pacific & Arctic Railway & Navigation Company in the United States.

1897, Apr. 23 —Incorporation of the British Columbia Yukon Railway Company in British Columbia.

1897, Jun. 29 —Incorporation of the British Yukon Mining, Trading & Transportation Company in Yukon Territory.

1898, July 20 —White Pass & Yukon Railway Company Limited organized in Great Britain to carry out charter rights and concessions of the three constituent companies.

1898, July 21 —First train operates for four miles out of Skagway.

1900 —British Yukon Mining, Trading & Transportation Company name changed to British Yukon Railway Company.

1900, Jun. 9 —Taku Tram purchased from John Irving Transportation Co., incorporated into WP&YR Ry. Co.

1900, July 29 —Last spike driven at Carcross completing line from Skagway to Whitehorse.

1900, Aug. 15 —Railway opened throughout from Skagway to Whitehorse.

1901 —British Yukon Navigation Company (BYN) incorporated to operate Taku Tram, and steamboat fleet in Yukon/Alaska.

1910, Aug —Branch completed from Pueblo to MacRae, YT.

1918 —Pueblo branch abandoned.

1942, Oct. 1 —WP&YR taken over by Transportation Corps, United States Army.

1946, Apr. 30 —Railway relinquished by United States Army.

1951, Sep. 4 —Incorporation in Canada of White Pass & Yukon Corporation Ltd., a holding Company, to acquire from WP&Y Ry. Co. Ltd. (in liquidation), assets and share capital of latter in three constituent companies listed above, plus the BYN, whose steamboats ceased operation in 1955.

1957 —WP&YR inaugurates container haulage service between Vancouver, BC, Whitehorse, other points, using a coastal freighter, the railway and fleet of trucks on Yukon and Alaska highway systems. This is pioneer application of integrated container service in North America.

1969, autumn —Main line south of White Pass diverted through tunnel, thus bypassing Dead Horse Gulch viaduct, a noted landmark and engineering feature.

1982 —Mines close, so regular train operations cease.

1988 —WP&YR reopens line Skagway, Alaska to Summit. as a passenger tourist railroad.

1989 —WP&YR opens line to Fraser and Bennett, BC for passenger traffic.

1992 —Due to low traffic, five diesel engines sold to Colombia.

1999 —WP&YR re-acquires five locomotives that had been sold to Colombia.

1999 —One steam locomotive, No. 73, in operation.

2000 —Back-up steam locomotive No. 40, originally from Guatemala, leased from Colorado. Found unsuitable; returned 2001.

2000, July —First passenger trains since 1982 (one is *"Golden Spike Centennial"* excursion) operate to Carcross, YT.

2004 —WP&YR rebuilding its heaviest locomotive No. 69, anticipating steam-hauled excursion in 2005.

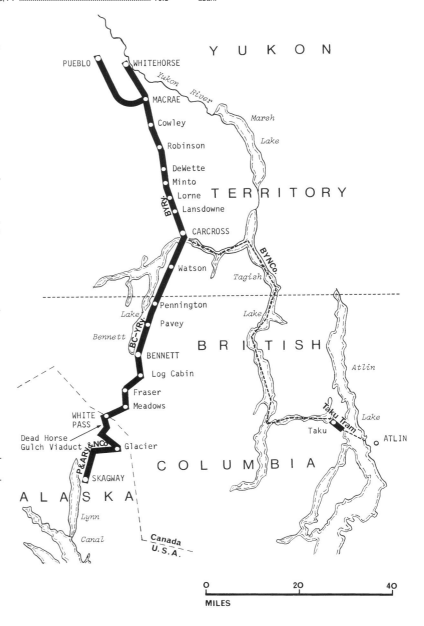

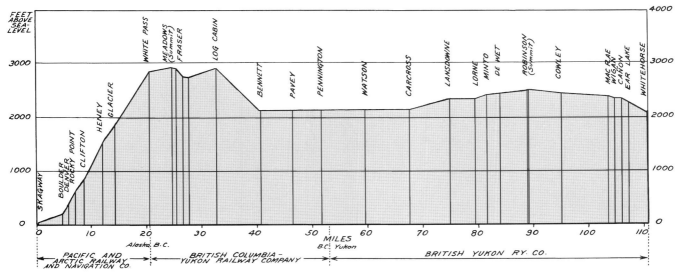

Coo/West collection

Previous pages: A double-headed passenger train is crossing a trestle and is about to enter a snow shed and tunnel on the WP&YR. This is typical of the terrain encountered by this railway.

ALAN THOMAS

Another "newer" addition to the WP&YR roster was this steel caboose, trailing an empty ore train past Skagway Cemetery in July 1970.

OMER LAVALLÉE

June 1959 view in White Pass & Yukon Route's Skagway yard.

OMER LAVALLÉE

Parlour cars outnumber other passenger rolling stock on the White Pass & Yukon Route. Car 236, "Lake Mayo", was photographed at Skagway in June 1959. Indistinguishable initials directly below name on car side are those of the WP&YR's Alaska constituent, the Pacific & Arctic Railway & Navigation Company.

WP&YR's first steam locomotive, originally No. 1 and later No. 51, is preserved at Whitehorse Museum.

White Pass & Yukon Route motive power of other years.

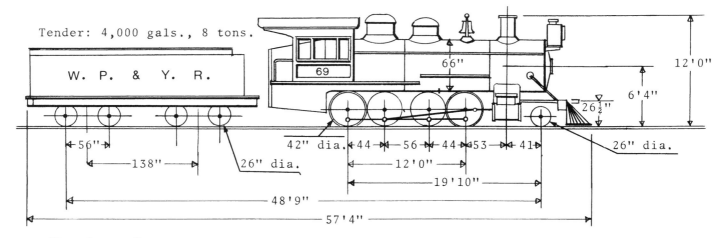

Tender: 4,000 gals., 8 tons.

W. P. & Y. R.

12'0"

66"

6'4"

26½"

56"

138"

26" dia.

42" dia.

44 — 56 — 44 — 53 — 41

12'0"

19'10"

26" dia.

48'9"

57'4"

Steam Locomotives

Nos. 1898 1900		Builder	Year	C/N	Type	Cyls.	Dri.	Notes
"Duchess"		Baldwin	9/1878	4424	2-4-0T	10x12"	27"	Built as an 0-6-0 for Wellington Colliery Railway, who regauged it from 30" to 36" circa mid-1880s. When altered, side-rods between leading and main drivers were not reapplied, leaving engine a 2-4-0T. Sold 1899 to John Irving Navigation Co., sold June 1900 to WP&YR. Preserved at Carcross, YT since 1936.
1/1	51	Brooks	1881		2-6-0	14x18"	42"	Acquired from Columbia & Puget Sound Rly. in 1898, originally Utah & Northern Rly. Now displayed at MacBride Museum, Whitehorse, YT.
1/2	52	"	"		"	"	"	Acquired from Columbia & Puget Sound Rly. in 1898, originally Utah & Northern Rly. Stored at Taku, BC from 1937 to 1963 when it was moved to Skagway, Alaska where it has been preserved by the Brotherhood of Railroad Trainmen and the Brotherhood of Locomotive Firemen and Enginemen.
1/3	53	Grant	8/1882		2-8-0	15½x20"	36"	Acquired from Columbia & Puget Sound Rly. in 1898. Scrapped at Seattle, WA in 1918.
1/4	54	Baldwin	3/1898	4294	4-4-0	12x16"	42"	Acquired from Columbia & Puget Sound Rly. in 1898. Sold to Tanana Valley Railway (Tanana Mines Railway) Alaska in 1905.
5	55	"	5/1885	7597	2-8-0	15x18"	36"	Acquired from Columbia & Puget Sound Rly. in 1898. Sold to Klondike Mines Rly. in 1905. Preserved at Dawson City Museum, Dawson City. YT.
6	56	"	1/1899	16455	"	19&11½x20"	38"	Acquired new in 1899 and converted to simple steam distribution in 1907. Scrapped in 1938.
7	57	"	"	16456	"	"	"	Acquired new in 1899. Sold to Klondike Mines Rly. in 1906. Preserved at Dawson City Museum, Dawson City. YT.
8	58	Climax	12/1897	167	3-trk.	14x14"	30"	Acquired from Pacific Contract Co. in 1900. Sold to Maytown Lumber Co. (Washington) in 1903. Claimed to be the only narrow gauge, three-truck Climax ever built.
	2/4	Baldwin	3/1912	37564	2-6-2	15x20"	37"	Acquired from Klondike Mines Rly. in 1942. Sold in 1955 to Oak Creek Central Tourist Railway, Oak Creek, WI 2001 Preserved at Wild's Game Farm, El Reno, OK.
	10*	"	1/1916	42766	4-6-0	16x22"	45"	Acquired by US Army Transportation Corps in 1942 from East Tennessee & Western North Carolina RR. Engine damaged in roundhouse fire at Skagway in 1943 and was scrapped at Seattle in 1945.
	14*	"	9/1919	52406	"	"	"	Acquired by US Army Transportation Corps in 1942 from East Tennessee & Western North Carolina RR. Engine damaged in roundhouse fire at Skagway in 1943 and was scrapped at Seattle in 1945.
	20*	"	12/1890	11355	2-8-0	16x20"	37"	Acquired by US Army Transportation Corps in 1943 from Colorado & Southern RR. Scrapped at Seattle in 1945.
	21*	"	"	11356	"	"	"	Acquired by US Army Transportation Corps in 1943 from Colorado & Southern RR. Scrapped at Seattle in 1945.
	22*	"	4/1904	24109	"	15x20"	"	Acquired by US Army Transportation Corps in 1943 from Silverton Northern RR. (Colorado). Scrapped at Seattle in 1945.
	23*	"	4/1906	27977	"	16x20"	"	Acquired by US Army Transportation Corps in 1943 from Silverton Northern RR. (Colorado). Scrapped at Seattle in 1945.
	24*	"	12/1904	24130	"	"	"	Acquired by US Army Transportation Corps in 1943 from Silverton Northern RR. (Colorado). Scrapped at Skagway in 1951.
	59	"	5/1900	17749	4-6-0	17x20"	42"	Acquired new in 1900. Scrapped in 1941.
	60	"	"	17750	"	"	"	Acquired new in 1900. Scrapped in 1949. Used as rip-rap at Mile 2.5 (Skagway River). Retrieved in 1988 and held at Skagway.
	61	"	6/1900	17814	2-8-0	"	38"	Acquired new in 1900. Scrapped in 1949. Used as rip-rap at Mile 2.5 (Skagway River). Retrieved in 1988 and held at Skagway.
	62	"	"	17895	4-6-0	17x22"	44"	Acquired new in 1900. Scrapped in 1949. Used as rip-rap at Mile 2.3 (Skagway River). Retrieved in 1988 and held at Skagway.
	63	Brooks	1881	522	2-6-0	14x18"	42"	Sold to Klondike Mines Rly. in 1902. Preserved at Dawson City Museum, Dawson City. YT.
	64			"		12x18"	33"	Scrapped in 1918.
	65			"		14x18"	42"	Sold to Tanana Valley Rly. (Alaska) in 1906.
	66	Baldwin	5/1901	18964	4-6-0	17x20"	"	Acquired new in 1901. Scrapped in 1967 and used as rip-rap at Mile 4.7 (Skagway River).
	67	"	"	18965	"	"	"	Acquired new in 1901. Retired in 1943. Used as rip-rap at unspecified location on Skagway River.
	68	"	6/1907	30998	2-8-0	19x22"	40"	Acquired new in 1907. Scrapped as result of hitting rock slide at Mile 15.6 in August 1917.
	69	"	6/1908	32962	"	21x22"	42"	Acquired new in 1908. Sold in 1956 to Black Hills Central Tourist Rly,, Hill City, SD—as "Klondike Casey". Subsequently located at Stuhr Museum of the Prairie Pioneer, Grand Island, Nebraska. Now being rebuilt for WP&YR steam excursions anticipated for 2005.
	70	"	5/1938	62234	2-8-2	17x22"	44"	Acquired new in 1938. Retired in 1963. Sold to Rebel RR and now preserved at Pigeon Forge, Tennessee.
	71	"	1/1939	62257	"	"	"	Acquired new in 1939. Retired in 1963. Sold to Rebel RR in 1977 and now preserved at Pigeon Forge, Tennessee.
	72	"	5/1947	73351	"	"	"	Acquired new in 1947. Retired in 1964, but used as stationary boiler. Damaged in fire at Skagway roundhouse in 1969. Remains now at Pigeon Forge, Tennessee.
	73	"	"	73352	"	"	"	Acquired new in 1947. Retired in 1964 and put on display at Bennett Museum, Bennett, BC in 1968. Restored to operating condition. Still in operation.
	80	Alco	5/1920	61980	"	19x20"	"	Acquired in 1940 from the Sumpter Valley RR. Retired in 1958. It is now at Railroad Park, Baker City, Oregon.
	81	"	"	61981	"	"	"	

WHITE PASS & YUKON ROUTE 2-8-0

Road Nos.	69
Gauge	36"
Type	2-8-0
Builder	BLW
Date	1908
Cylinders (diam. & stroke)	21"x22"
Driving Wheels	42"
Pressure	160 p.s.i.
Tractive Effort	24,000 lbs.

Weights (working order)
On drivers	120,000 lbs.
Total engine	133,000 lbs.
Tender	80,000 lbs.

Tender Capacity
Coal	8 tons
Water	4,000 gals.
Oil	—

Ex US Army 2-8-2 No. 190, pictured out of service at Skagway in 1959, was sold to a tourist railway in North Carolina in 1960, and is now named "Yukon Queen". These locomotives were originally built for military use on metre-gauge.

Steam Locomotives

Nos. 1898 1900	Builder	Year	C/N	Type	Cyls.	Dri.	Notes
190*	Baldwin	2/1943	69425	2-8-2	16x24"	48"	Acquired new in 1943 by US Army Transportation Corps. Transferred to WP&YR in 1945. It was sold in 1960 to the Tweetsie Tourist Railway, Blowing Rock, NC.
191*	"	"	68426	"	"	"	Acquired new in 1943 by US Army Transportation Corps. Transferred to WP&YR in 1945. Scrapped in 1951.
192*	"	"	69427	"	"	"	Acquired new in 1943 by US Army Transportation Corps. Transferred to WP&YR in 1945. Sold in 1961 to the Rebel RR and now preserved at Pigeon Forge, Tennessee.
193*	"	"	69428	"	"	"	Acquired new in 1943 by US Army Transportation Corps. Transferred to WP&YR in 1945. Scrapped in 1951.
194*	"	"	69429	"	"	"	Acquired new in 1943 by US Army Transportation Corps. Transferred to WP&YR in 1945. Scrapped in 1951.
195*	"	"	69430	"	"	"	Acquired new in 1943 by US Army Transportation Corps. Transferred to WP&YR in 1945. Now displayed at Trail of '98 Museum, Skagway.
196*	"	"	69431	"	"	"	Acquired new in 1943 by US Army Transportation Corps. Transferred to WP&YR in 1945. Retired in 1961 and in 1968 used as rip-rap at Mile 4.7 (Skagway River).
197*	"	"	69432	"	"	"	Acquired new in 1943 by US Army Transportation Corps. Transferred to WP&YR in 1945. Scrapped in 1951.
198*	"	"	69433	"	"	"	Acquired new in 1943 by US Army Transportation Corps. Scrapped at Seattle in 1944.
199*	"	"	69434	"	"	"	Acquired new in 1943 by US Army Transportation Corps. Scrapped at Seattle in 1944.
200*	"	"	69435	"	"	"	Acquired new in 1943 by US Army Transportation Corps. Scrapped at Seattle in 1944.
250*	Alco	9/1923	64981	"	18x22"	"	Acquired by US Army Transportation Corps. in 1942 from D&RGW (#470). Scrapped at Seattle in 1944.
251*	"	"	64982	"	"	"	Acquired by US Army Transportation Corps. in 1942 from D&RGW (#471). Scrapped at Seattle in 1945.
252*	"	"	64983	"	"	"	Acquired by US Army Transportation Corps. in 1942 from D&RGW (#472). Scrapped at Ogden in 1945.
253*	"	"	64985	"	"	"	Acquired by US Army Transportation Corps. in 1942 from D&RGW (#474). Scrapped at Seattle in 1945.
254*	"	"	64986	"	"	"	Acquired by US Army Transportation Corp. in 1942 from D&RGW (#475). Scrapped at Seattle in 1945.
255*	"	"	64988	"	"	"	Acquired by US Army Transportation Corp. in 1942 from D&RGW (#477). Scrapped at Seattle in 1945.
256*	"	"	64990	"	"	"	Acquired by US Army Transportation Corps. in 1942 from D&RGW (#479). Scrapped at Seattle in 1945.

Resplendent No. 73, White Pass & Yukon Route's last steam locomotive, at Skagway shop in June 1959.

Twenty-ton Plymouth yard engine No. 3, built in 1942, was a casualty of a fire which destroyed the Skagway shops in 1969.

WP&YR engine No. 90 arrives at Whitehorse with daily train, Both photos taken in June 1959.

WP&YR Engine 104, an Alco/MLW product of 1969, is shown here loaded for shipment to the west coast.

Internal Combustion Locomotives

No.	Builder	Year	C/N	Type	Weight	H.P.	Notes
2/1	GE	1947		B	25 tons	150	Acquired in 1969 from Colorado Fuel & Iron Co., Pueblo, Colorado to replace No. 2/3. Retired in 1981. To BC Forest Museum, Duncan, BC in 1985.
2/2	"	1947		"	25 "	"	Acquired in 1969 from Colorado Fuel & Iron Co., Pueblo, Colorado. Retired in 1981, scrapped in North Vancouver 1985.
2/3	Plymouth	1942	4471	"	20 "	175	Acquired in 1942 from US Army. Destroyed in roundhouse fire at Skagway October 15, 1969.
90	GE	6/1954	32060	C-C	84 "	930	Acquired new in 1954. Still in service.
91	"	"	32061	"	84 "	"	Acquired new in 1954. Still in service.
92	"	12/1956	32709	"	86 "	"	Acquired new in 1956. Still in service.
93	"	"	32710	"	86 "	"	Acquired new in 1956. Still in service.
94	"	"	32711	"	86 "	"	Acquired new in 1956. Still in service.
95	"	3/1963	34592	"	84 "	"	Acquired new in 1963. Still in service.
96	"	"	34593	"	84 "	"	Acquired new in 1963. Taken out of service after 1976 fire. Used for parts. Rebuilt 2003, returned to active service.
97	"	"	34594	"	84 "	"	Acquired new in 1963. Still in service.
98	"	5/1966	35790	"	85 "	990	Acquired new in 1966. Still in service.
99	"	"	35791	"	85 "	"	Acquired new in 1966. Still in service.
100	"	"	35792	"	85 "	"	Acquired new in 1966. Still in service.
101	Alco	6/1969	6023-01	"	105 "	1200	Acquired new in 1969. Sold in 1992 to Sociedad Colombiana de Transporte Ferroviario (Colombia). Re-acquired by WP&YR in 1999. Still in service.
102	"	"	6023-02	"	105 "	"	Acquired new in 1969. Destroyed in roundhouse fire at Skagway October 15, 1969.
103	"	"	6023-03	"	105 "	"	Acquired new in 1969. Sold in 1992 to Sociedad Colombiana de Transporte Ferroviario (Colombia). Re-acquired by WP&YR in 1999. Stored inactive at Skagway Yard in Colombia paint scheme.
104	"	"	6023-04	"	105 "	"	Acquired new in 1969. Sold in 1992 to Sociedad Colombiana de Transporte Ferroviario (Colombia). Re-acquired by WP&YR in 1999. Still in service.
105	"	"	6023-05	"	105 "	"	Acquired new in 1969. Destroyed in roundhouse fire at Skagway October 15, 1969.
106	"	"	6023-06	"	105 "	"	Acquired new in 1969. Sold in 1992 to Sociedad Colombiana de Transporte Ferroviario (Colombia). Re-acquired by WP&YR in 1999. Still in service.
107	"	"	6023-07	"	105 "	"	Acquired new in 1969. Sold in 1992 to Sociedad Colombiana de Transporte Ferroviario (Colombia). Re-acquired by WP&YR in 1999. Still in service.
108	"	12/1971	6054-01	"	105 "	"	Acquired new in 1971. Still in service.
109	"	"	6054-02	"	105 "	"	Acquired new in 1971. Still in service.
110	"	"	6054-03	"	105 "	"	Acquired new in 1971. Still in service.
111	MLW/Bombardier	9/1982	6123-01	"	108 "	"	Completed by Bombardier in 1982. Stored in Montreal area until 1993 when sold to US Gypsum, Plaster City, California to replace wrecked 113.
112	"	"	6123-02	"	108 "	"	Completed by Bombardier in 1982. Stored in Montreal area until 1991 when sold to US Gypsum, Plaster City, California.
113	"	"	6123-03	"	108 "	"	Completed by Bombardier in 1982. Stored in Montreal area until 1991 when sold to US Gypsum, Plaster City, California where destroyed in wreck
114	"	"	6123-04	"	108 "	"	Completed by Bombardier in 1982. Stored in Montreal area until 1995 when shipped to Skagway. Still in service.

Self-Propelled Units

No.	Builder	Year	C/N	Type	Notes
No #	WIW	1937	68	Ford V-8 Engine	Acquired new in 1937. Used on Taku Tram Division of WP&YR 1937-1950; at WP&YR tie plant, Carcross YT, 1953-1982; stored at Whitehorse YT, 1982-1992. Rebuilt in 1993 and used as yard engine at Skagway. Now retired.
5	Beartown	1998	—	Diesel-Hydraulic Railbus 450-hp Engine	Acquired new in 1998. Performance unsatisfactory. Now used as coach towed behind engine.

The incongruity of a mixed train pulling containers as well as open-platformed, wooden passenger cars is well shown in this picture of WP&YR trains meeting at the station and dining room at Bennett, British Columbia. Cars in foreground are part of northbound No. 1; No.2, headed by two 90 series engines, will leave shortly for Skagway, Alaska.

Facing page: Southbound excursion train No. 22, headed by engines 93 and 94, on Bridge 15C June 18th 1995.

Steaming southbound towards Skagway, locomotive No. 73 is crossing bridge 7C at mile 7.6, almost directly across the Skagway River canyon from the US Customs Station which is situated on the South Klondike Highway.

Exiting the tunnel's south portal onto Bridge 15C spanning Glacier Gorge, is a Summit excursion train on June 18th 1995. The motive power was composed of the three then-remaining 100-Class engines: Nos. 109, 110 and 108.

Engines 92 and 100 haul June 24th 1991 Summit excursion train across the east fork of the Skagway River on Bridge 5A. No. 92 is in the 1981-82 blue-and-white paint scheme, which reverted to the original yellow-and-green thereafter.

Train No. 2 at Clifton overhang, mile 8.5, on July 10th 1993. The motive power was provided by engines 97 and 98. Located beneath a giant rock overhang, this was a popular location for photographers.

ERIC JOHNSON

The original Cut-off Gulch Bridge 18A appears prominently as engines 94 and 93 ease WP&YR train No. 22 across the "new" bridge on June 17th 1995. The original, in the left foreground, was built in 1901 and abandoned in 1969.

DON MCQUEEN

Engines 90 and 97 power train No. 6, traveling southbound to Skagway on July 14th 1977. Starting in 1977, this short-lived blue-white-and-red paint scheme was applied to only ten active diesel engines, but the entire fleet of active diesels was repainted to solid-blue-with-white in 1980-81. Photographer Don McQueen is aboard train No. 1, which is north-bound to Whitehorse with engines 104 and 106 as power. No. 1 is in the Log Cabin siding, allowing No. 6 to pass.

June 17th 1995 saw train No. 31 with engines 110 and 108 observing the 12 mph speed restriction over the Cut-Off Gulch Bridge. The original Bridge 18A is in the background.

Train No. 22 northbound to Fraser, British Columbia, sporting engines 91, 90 and 95, handled by engineer John Westfall, is seen at mile 23.6 on June 20th 1995. Snow fences to reduce drifting across the tracks, are visible in the background.

The Thompson River is spanned by Bridge 26A as train No. 22 with engines 98 and 90 crosses over on June 11th 1995, headed for Skagway. Patches of snow remain on the mountains.

A maintenance-of-way track motor car and trailer is seen rolling through Fraser, British Columbia on June 21st 1991. The Canada Customs station is behind the cars (note the Canadian flag), between the northbound and southbound lanes of the South Klondike Highway.

On June 16th 1995, engineer John Westfall guides train No. 23 as it approaches Fraser, bound for Bennett, British Columbia, ready to bypass southbound engines 94 and 93 with worktrain waiting at Fraser station.

The scenery is spectacular alongside Fraser Lake as train No. 24 passes with engines 91 and 90 on June 19th 1995, southbound from Bennett, British Columbia.

NARROW GAUGE RAILWAYS OF CANADA

This Cooke rotary plow was originally built in 1898 and retired six decades later. After using bulldozers for snow-clearing from the 1960s to 1995, the plow was rebuilt and returned to work. It is seen working north of White Pass on April 29th 1996.

On August 30th 1997, southbound train is hauling cupola-outfitted baggage / coach No. 211 and flat car No. 479. This is a Lake Bennett excursion. The lead coaches carry the round-trip passengers, while car No. 211 carries the conductor, the returning Chilkoot Pass trekkers, and their back-packs.

Baldwin No. 73, assisted by engines 93 and 97, passes through once-very-busy Log Cabin on July 8th 1993, returning from Bennett, British Columbia.

Baldwin-built locomotive "The Duchess" has been on display at Carcross, Yukon Territory since the 1930s. Although it never operated on the WP&YR, it did operate on its Taku Tram subsidiary between 1900 and 1921.

NARROW GAUGE RAILWAYS OF CANADA

DEDMAN'S PHOTO, COURTESY WP&YR

Engines 100 and 99 head the train unloading passengers at Skagway Station behind and to the right. (The former station is above, centre.) Then, after uncoupling, the two engines will cross Broadway, reversing on the foreground siding, to re-couple at the train's opposite end and load Summit-bound passengers.

CHRISTIAN RACICA, COURTESY WP&YR

Baldwin-built locomotive No. 73 awaits loading of passengers for return to Skagway from Bennett, British Columbia, located in International Klondike Gold Rush Historical Park. The station's original south dining room has been restored, with displays depicting area history.

CHRISTIAN RACICA, COURTESY WP&YR

On bridge 15A, a northbound train is approaching Slippery Rock (mile 15.6), so named because of difficulty in blasting the grade which was cut from the near-vertical cliff face that begins in the foreground. In the distance can be seen rail grade, several hundred feet lower in elevation, at about mile 14, south of Glacier.

ERIC JOHNSON

On June 16th 1995, engines 91 and 90 cut off the Lake Bennett Adventure/Chilkoot hiker's Train No. 23 on the Bennett station (main) track. They ran to the north switch, returned on the passing (centre) track, and recoupled, ready to depart southbound for Skagway as train No. 24. Buildings in the background are mainly for maintenance of way crews, since no one lives in Bennett now. Equipment is stored on the lake-side siding, and the old loop track—very necessary when rotary snow plows were in use—can be seen at the extreme right (east) side.

ERIC JOHNSON

Further south, train No. 24 approaches Fraser station with coach No. 220, "Lake Bennett", behind the locomotives. Note the water tank on the left side of the track well ahead of the train, the Fraser siding to the right (west) of the main line, and Fraser Lake to the left of the train. Barely visible across the tracks from the water tank, and straddling the South Klondike Highway, is the Canada Customs station. Fraser, at mile 27.7, is also the transfer point for the train/bus traffic between Skagway and Whitehorse. The buses park in the open lot between the water tank and the lake. A storage track is barely visible between the siding and the foreground bushes.

Returning to Skagway from Fraser, British Columbia, the twice-daily train exits the 250-foot tunnel through Tunnel Mountain at Mile 15.85, onto Bridge 15C to cross Glacier Gorge, 1000 feet below.

Soon after Spring inauguration of the new tour season, steam locomotive No. 73 pulls away from the passenger cruise-ship Broadway Dock. For much of the 1990s, No. 73 took only the scheduled first morning excursion to Summit. It then took the first afternoon excursion from the docks (to satisfy steam enthusiasts with cameras) to the shops, where diesels took over for the haul to the Summit on many days.

Engineer Gilbert Thompson spots No. 5 for water on August 4th 1956. The ancient water tower was replaced the following year. Note the contemporary Studebaker automobile.

In the summer of 1953, passengers had just detrained from the "large car" and are boarding MS "Iroquois II" which succeeded the steamers.

Idyllic scene midway on the 1.1-mile line showing empty train returning to South Portage, 1958.

H&LB Engine 5 and train wait beside the wharf at South Portage.

Locomotive No. 5 with its train is about to cross the dirt road near North Portage, Peninsula Lake, Ontario on August 4th 1956.

At South Portage the Tour Boat "Purser" who doubled as Conductor for the rail journey, talks to bystanders in the summer of 1953. He wears his uniform even though the steamers had disappeared the previous year.

•17•

Huntsville, Lake of Bays & Lake Simcoe Railway & Navigation Company

IT WAS IN 1902 THAT A TANNERY AT Huntsville, Ontario, caused a 1⅛-mile tramway to be built connecting Peninsula Lake and Lake of Bays, bridging a navigation gap in an otherwise all-water system extending east of Huntsville into the forests of what is now Algonquin Park. The steamers plying these lakes hauled tanbark to the tannery, and at the South Portage, on Lake of Bays, it was this product which was loaded into the diminutive train, and pulled over to Peninsula Lake at North Portage, where it was loaded on a vessel for the remainder of the trip to Huntsville. This carrier was built to the strange gauge of 3'8½".

Later, as the importance of the tannery diminished, and the development of the Huntsville area as a playground grew, the railway started to haul passengers in connection with a steamer service, the whole being operated by the Huntsville, Lake of Bays and Lake Simcoe Railway & Navigation Company. The railway, however, was usually known as the "Portage Railway" and attained a considerable measure of fame as a tourist attraction. It did not, of course, function in winter, and passengers were loaded into two ancient, open-bench, former electric streetcars, now mounted on narrow gauge trucks.

In 1951, the railway acquired two newer saddle-tank engines to replace the originals which had been in use since the line opened. The new additions, however, had a track gauge of 3'6", and choosing the lesser of two evils, the railway gauge was narrowed 2½"

R. J. SANDUSKY

Locomotive No. 5 and train at switch back, North Portage in Ontario's "cottage country" lake district during 1958. Note stub switch.

Her bell at a jaunty angle, H&LB No. 5 waits at South Portage on August 22nd 1953.

H&LB No. 5 awaits the docking of M.S. "Iroquois II" at North Portage on August 16th 1958. This was the boat's last season and the second to last for the railway.

H&LB Engine No. 5 is on its northbound trip through the forest beside Osborne's Lake enroute to North Portage on August 16th 1958.

Train and "Terminal" at South Portage, with Lake of Bays in background, 1959.

and the rolling stock changed accordingly. One of the engines, No. 7, was considered to be too heavy for operation and it was never used.

The railway's last season was that of 1959. Early in 1963, the locomotives, cars and track were sold to Mr. Percy Broadbear who built a line in Pinafore Park, St. Thomas, Ontario for tourist purposes. This equipment was returned to Huntsville in 1985 where it was placed on display under the auspices of the Huntsville & Lake of Bays Railway Society.

July 1st 2000 saw the return to operation of the former H&LB equipment. It provides a tourist attraction at Muskoka Heritage Place in Huntsville. Prior to this, some consideration had been given to restoring operation in the original location of the railway between Lake of Bays and Peninsula Lake. Studies, however, indicated that difficulty of access for tourists would render such an enterprise unfeasible and the idea was dropped.

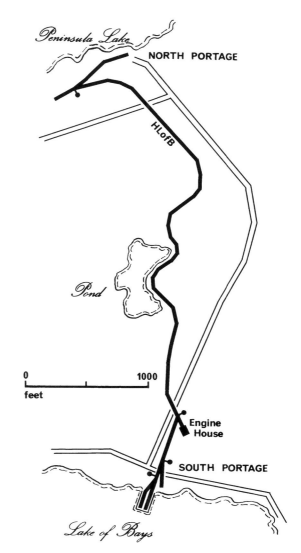

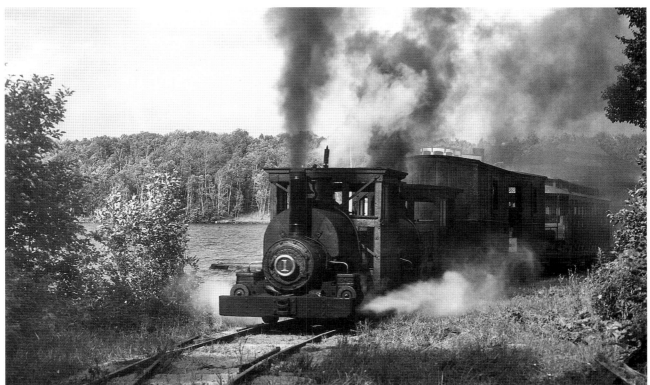

Locomotive Nos. 1 and 2 making an energetic start from South Portage in the 1930s. Note light rail on track which was exactly one foot narrower than standard gauge at this period.

The sway-backed baggage car is remarkable in this photograph of H&LB No. 2 leaving South Portage, date unknown.

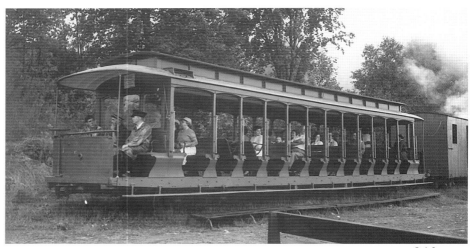

Jackson & Sharp outshopped the Portage Railway's "large car" originally for an electric line in New Jersey.

The "small car" was once an open-bench standard gauge electric car on the Toronto Suburban Railway.

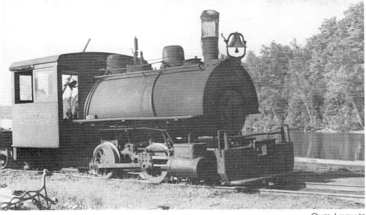

OMER LAVALLÉE

Locomotive No. 5 at South Portage, 1958.

LATE W. G. COLE

Locomotive Nos. 1 and 2 at South Portage, 1944.

R. J. SANDUSKY

Locomotive No. 7 in engine house at South Portage. Note window in building obviously salvaged from one of the steamships. Due to excessive weight, No. 7 was never used.

Huntsville, Lake of Bays & Lake Simcoe Railway & Navigation Company
Also known as the "Portage Railway"

South Portage (Lake of Bays) to
North Portage (Peninsula Lake), Ont. .... 1.1 miles   aban.

Gauge: 3 feet, 8½ inches until 1948. 3 feet, 6 inches after 1948.

Chronology:

c1902	—Railway built from North Portage on Peninsula Lake, to South Portage on Lake of Bays, in Muskoka District of Ontario, as a portage in a water route hauling tanbark to tannery at Huntsville, Ont.
	—Passenger service later undertaken exclusively.
1948	—Gauge changed from 3'8½" to 3'6" as a result of acquisition of newer motive power to replace original locomotives.
1958, Sep.	—Operation discontinued for season, but not subsequently resumed.
1963, June	—Line's assets sold to Percy Broadbear, London, Ont., who removed engines, rolling stock and rails and reinstalled part of line in Pinafore Park, St. Thomas, Ont. as an amusement railway.

Steam Locomotives

No.	Builder	Year	C/N	Type	Cyls.	Dri.	From	To	Notes
1/1	Porter	1888	911	0-4-0T	7x14"		E. B. Eddy Co. 1905	Retired 1948	A
1/2	"	"	912	"	"		" "	"	A
2/1	Montreal	1926	66948	"	9x14"		C.G.Co. #5 1948	6/63 P. Broadbear	B
2/2	"	"	67167	"	10x16"		" #7 "	" "	C

Notes:

A—Purchased from E. B. Eddy Co., Hull, Que. in 1905. Sold in 1949 to Cameron Peck of Chicago and now on display at the Harold Warp Pioneer Village, Minden, Nebraska.

B—Acquired from Canadian Gypsum Co., Nova Scotia and assigned H&LofB. # which was not applied. Railway line was regauged to accommodate the new motive power. In 1963 was acquired by Pinafore Park, St. Thomas, Ont. and in 1985 was moved to Huntsville, Ont.

C—Same as C.G.Co. #5. This engine was too heavy to operate on the H&LofB line and was never used.

Rolling Stock

Included two former open-bench electric streetcars, de-motored and mounted on n.g. double trucks. One was DT car from Atlantic City built by Jackson & Sharp, Wilmington, Delaware. Other was ST car from Toronto Suburban Railway built by Toronto Railway Co.

Note: —During career as a passenger carrier, this railway operated only in summer months and in connection with boat cruise services on the adjacent lakes. In latter years, boat service was limited to Peninsula Lake only and passengers were taken for a round trip on the "Portage Railway" to South Portage and immediate return.

Klondike Mines Railway

SIX YEARS AFTER THE OPENING OF THE White Pass & Yukon Route between Skagway and Whitehorse, the Yukon was the scene of construction of a second narrow gauge railway, whose operations were, however, short-lived.

This company, the Klondike Mines Railway Company, was incorporated in 1899 to build from Klondike City, via Bonanza Creek and Indian River to the Divide. Construction did not get under way until 1905, however, and the whole operation was financed by a British company, the Dawson, Grand Forks & Stewart River Railway Company, of London, England. Fifteen miles of the 80 miles projected were completed in 1905, and in November, 1906, the

Klondike Mines Railway was opened between Dawson City and Sulphur Spring, 31.81 miles. At this point, construction stopped, and limited operation was carried on over the completed section, using two 2-6-0s and one 2-8-0 type steam locomotives which had been purchased from the White Pass & Yukon Route. A fourth locomotive, a 2-6-2, was acquired new from Baldwin in 1912. It was this locomotive that was taken by the WP&YR in 1942.

Despite its name, the Klondike Mines Railway's principal traffic was in merchandise and lumber, and it had no mineral traffic to speak of. Operation ceased in the autumn of 1913, after only seven years' service, and the four locomotives, two passenger cars, and

One of the first trains to take Yukon excursionists over the Klondike Mines Railway operated on September 30th 1905, comprising a 2-6-0 locomotive, passenger coach and two flatcars hastily fitted up to accommodate the overflow.

General view of Yukon's Dawson City (background) and Klondike City (foreground) about 1920. Two Klondike Mines Railway passenger cars and a string of flat cars lie derelict in the foreground. The three locomotives, now on display in Dawson, were hauled over the frozen ice of the Stewart River from Klondike City in the winter of 1960-61.

Brooks built this locomotive in 1881 for the Kansas Central Railway. Klondike Mines Railway No. 1 is now on exhibit at Dawson City, Yukon.

A wood train on the Klondike Mines Railway passes through Klondike City, known more descriptively, if less elegantly, as "Lousetown". Dawson City is in the background, across the Klondike River.

some box and flat cars were abandoned at Dawson City. After remaining at the site of the old terminal for forty-eight years, three of the locomotives, which had suffered less from long neglect and exposure than might have been expected, were moved into Dawson City in the spring of 1961, for restoration and display as historical artifacts. The 2-8-0, a Vauclain compound with outside frames, is the only remaining compound steam locomotive in Canada. The fourth locomotive was rehabilitated and operated by the WP&YR to meet wartime traffic needs.

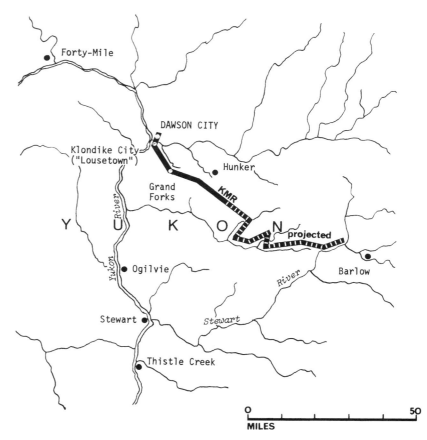

The Klondike line's enginehouse was strategically situated beside the local brewery.

CARL MULVIHILL

Klondike Mines Railway No. 3 is an outside-frame Baldwin-built Vauclain compound 2-8-0, formerly White Pass & Yukon Route No. 57, for which company it was built in 1899. It is the only remaining compound locomotive in Canada.

BALDWIN LOCOMOTIVE WORKS

Klondike Mines No. 4, built 1912, was "retrieved" by the White Pass & Yukon Route in 1942 and put back into service.

Klondike Mines Railway Company

Klondike City (opposite Dawson City) to Sulphur Spring (Hunker Summit), YT .... 31.81 miles aban.

Gauge: 3 feet, 0 inches.

Chronology:

1899	—Incorporation of Klondike Mines Railway Company.
1906, Nov	—Railway completed between Klondike City and Sulphur Spring, and operation commenced.
1915	—Service discontinued.

Steam Locomotives

No.	Builder	Year	C/N	Type	Cyls.	Dri.	From		To	Notes
1	Brooks	1881	522	2-6-0	12x18"	33"?	WP&YR	#63 1902	Retired 1915	A
2	Baldwin	1885	7597	2-8-0	15x18"	36"	"	#55 1904	"	A
3	"	1899	16456	"	11½x19x20"	38"	"	#57 1906	"	A,B
4	"	1912	37564	2-6-2	15x20"	37"	New		"	C

Notes: All locomotives were abandoned at Klondike City from 1915 onward.

A—Nos. 1, 2 and 3 were moved across the ice between Klondike City and Dawson City early in 1961 and preserved in Minto Park in Dawson City by Dawson Visitors' Association.

B—No. 3 is a Vauclain compound, the only compound locomotive extant in Canada.

C—No. 4 was taken out by the White Pass & Yukon Route in 1942 and used on WP&YR as 2/4. See WP&YR notes for further disposition.

•19•
Lenora Mount Sicker Copper Company

WHILE NEVER OFFICIALLY CHARTERED AS a common-carrier railway, the 36-inch gauge line of the Lenora Mount Sicker Copper Company, on Vancouver Island, which functioned between 1901 and 1907, carried passengers occasionally.

The line was opened from Lenora Mines to Mount Sicker siding on the Esquimalt & Nanaimo Railway, a distance of 6½ miles, on January 21st 1901. In July of the following year, it was extended a further five miles to Crofton, on the coast, using a route over the shoulder of Mount Richards which employed three switchbacks. The railway was laid with extremely light rail, 20 and 28 lbs. to the yard, contrasted with forty-pound and heavier rail used on other narrow gauge systems. The ruling grade, on the upper or Lenora section of the line, was some 700 feet to the mile, or thirteen percent, at what was known locally as "Haggerty Hill". It is no wonder that the railway used Shay-geared locomotives exclusively! The principal traffic was ore, and operations were suspended in 1907, after the Lenora Mine closed down. The railway lay dormant for five years, and was dismantled in 1912, except for a short section which was used for some time afterward by the Westholme Lumber Company.

Motive power consisted of three Shay-geared locomotives, and rolling stock numbered eight ore cars and two flat cars. Details of passenger equipment are not known, though its annual reports indicate that passengers were carried.

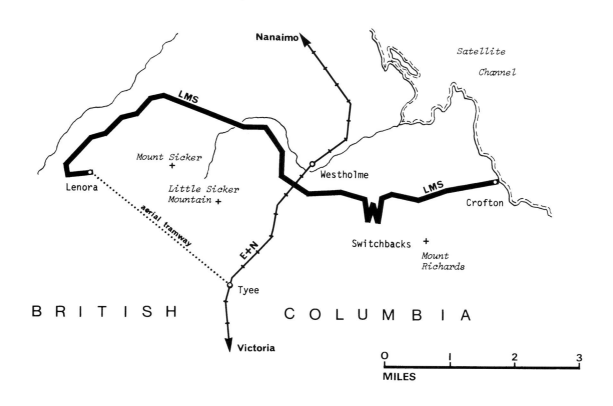

Curves and grades characterized the Lenora Mount Sicker Copper Company's railway on Vancouver Island, British Columbia. Here, a Shay and two cars make up an ore train.

Lenora Mount Sicker Copper Company

Lenora Mines to Crofton, BC .... 11.03 miles aban.

Gauge: 3 feet, 0 inches.

Chronology:

1901, Jan. 21 —Railway opened from Lenora Mines to Mount Sicker siding on the Esquimalt & Nanaimo Railway, 6¼ miles.

1902, spring —Railway extended from Mount Sicker siding to Crofton, BC.

1904 —Operations suspended and line abandoned.

Steam Locomotives

No.	Builder	Year	C/N	Type	Cyls.	Tons	From	To	Notes
1	Lima	1900	621	2-tr. Shay	6x10"	8½	New	H. M.Ellis Co.	A
2	"	1888	220	"	8x8"	18	HS&ECo. 1902	W. L.Co. 1906	B
3	"	1902	703	"	8x10"	21	"	" 1912	C

Notes:

A—Sold to H. M. Ellis Co., Lombard, BC after 1904.

B—Originally built for H. W. Sage Company in USA, engine bought second hand from Hoffius Steel & Equipment Co., Seattle, Wash. In 1906, it was acquired by Westholme Lumber Company which used part of LMSCCo. railway.

C—Engine wrecked after line closed but in 1912 it was rescued and repaired by Westholme Lumber Company. LMSCCo. also operated a standard gauge Forney, #4 on related section of line.

St. John's Street Railway Company

Newfoundland Light & Power Company

THE MOST EASTERLY STREET RAILWAY IN North America sums up the noteworthy feature of the tramway in St. John's, Newfoundland. In 1898, the government of Newfoundland entered into a contract with R. G. Reid & Company, which had just completed the building of the overland railway from Placentia Junction to Port-aux-Basques, whereby it was agreed that a new company, to be known as the Reid-Newfoundland Company, would operate the various railways owned by the government, and certain other public utilities, including an electric street railway in St. John's.

Work on the St. John's Street Railway started late in the following year, and on May 1st 1900, regular service started on Water Street. The line extended from the intersection with Topsail and Waterford Bridge roads in the west end, to Hill o' Chips in the east end, a distance of 1¾ miles. The car barn was just off Water Street at the corner of Job's Bridge Road and opposite the site of the now preserved railway station. At that time, the railway station and shops were at Fort William in the east end, where the Newfoundland Hotel is now. The line on Water Street was double track, with very light grooved rails and the Newfoundland gauge of 3'6" was used.

A year later, on May 7th 1901, three other lines were completed and opened for traffic. The Belt Line started at the east end, climbed up Hill o' Chips, Ordnance Street and Military Road to the summit at Rawlin's Cross then descended the hill by Queens Road and joined the main line at the foot of Adelaide Street near the Post Office. The LeMarchant line

A narrow gauge Ottawa-built Birney car heading westward up Military Road in St. John's, Newfoundland in this photo taken from the Newfoundland Hotel in the 1930s.

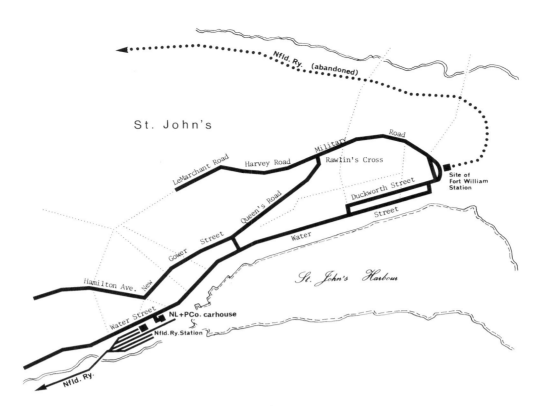

started from Rawlin's Cross and ran westward along Harvey Road and LeMarchant Road to the head of Barter's Hill. The Hamilton line ran westward from Adelaide Street on New Gower Street and Hamilton Avenue to the corner of Leslie Street. From the Belt Line, at the head of Ordnance Street, there was a spur into the shops of the Newfoundland Railway and for a year or two the cars were repaired in the railway shops.

Results did not come up to expectations and after a year, service was discontinued on the LeMarchant Road and Hamilton Avenue lines. The Water Street and Belt Line were combined and cars starting from Water Street west ran east, then around the Belt to Adelaide Street, and then returned by the same route. After World War I, the Reids gradually withdrew from their various enterprises in Newfoundland and in 1923, the St. John's Street Railway was sold to the

LATE ROBERT R. BROWN; COURTESY OF R. DOUGLAS BROWN

Early view of Water Street in St. John's, with La Rivière-built car of the St. John's Street Railway Company.

Newfoundland Light & Power Company. Plans were made to rehabilitate the property and in 1925, the line was completely rebuilt with heavier rails and new cars were bought. Instead of the double track on Water Street, there was a single track with turnouts but oddly enough the track was off centre and the second trolley wire was left aloft for over twenty years. There were two minor relocations: Hill o' Chips was dangerously steep so the new line left Water Street and turned up a lane just west of the War Memorial and then ran east on Duckworth Street, and instead of turning up Ordnance Street, it went on the opposite side of a little park and passed in front of the Newfoundland Hotel which had been erected on the site of the old Fort William station as it was known.

New Ottawa-built safety car No. 12 of the Newfoundland Light & Power Company, stands outside St. John's carhouse shortly after delivery.

During World War II, the street railway operated under very difficult conditions; minor collisions were frequent during the complete black-out, maintenance had to be neglected and the traffic was greatly in excess of the normal capacity of the equipment. In the extremely damp climate, the steel in the car bodies had gradually rusted away and it was said that only the many coats of paint kept the cars from falling apart.

Plans were made to replace the railway with a modern trolley bus service, but in the meantime, the city allowed the establishment of a rival in the form of an aggressive but inferior bus service. As a consequence, on September 15th 1948, the Newfoundland Light & Power Company quit the transportation field and abandoned the street railway. Like many other communities, St. John's had good reason to mourn the passing of the little red Birney cars.

What is probably the whole uniformed platform staff of the St. John's Street Railway pre-empted the windows and side of car No. 7 in the first years of the 20th century. The shop staff found places on the roof, aided by the stepladder barely in sight at right.

Remember when theatres featured illustrated songs along with motion pictures? You don't? Never mind; the advertiser was probably satisfied with the coverage provided by St. John's Street Railway No. 3.

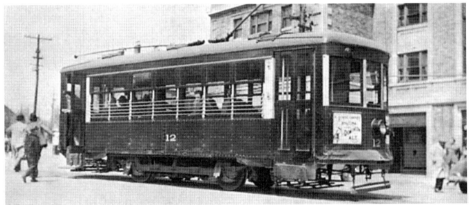

Ottawa-built Birney cars of the Newfoundland Light & Power Company had both doors on same side of car. Passengers embarked and disembarked on same side of street irrespective of direction car was travelling.

Newfoundland Light & Power Company

Street railway in and around City of St. John's, Nfld.

Gauge: 3 feet, 6 inches.

Chronology:

1898	—Construction of street railway in St. John's undertaken by Reid-Newfoundland Company in contract with Newfoundland government.
1899	—Physical construction started on St. John's Street Railway.
1900, May 1	—Regular service inaugurated on Water Street.
1901, May 7	—Regular service started on Belt Line, LeMarchant line and Hamilton line.
1902	—LeMarchant and Hamilton lines abandoned and Belt Line integrated with Water Street line.
1923	—St. John's Street Railway sold to Newfoundland Light & Power Company.
1925	—Lines rebuilt with minor relocations.
1948, Sep.15	—Street railway service in St. John's abandoned completely.

Electric Cars

No.	Builder	Year	Type	From	To	Notes
1	Lariviere, Montreal	1900	ST DE Closed	New	x c1926	
2	"	"	"	"	"	
3	"	"	"	"	"	
4	"	"	"	"	"	
5	"	"	"	"	"	
6	"	"	"	"	"	
7	"	"	"	"	"	
8	"	"	"	"	"	
9	McGuire-Cummings	"	DT DE Sweeper	"	x 1948	A
10	Ottawa Car Mfg. Co.	1926	ST DE Birney Safety Car	"	"	
11	"	"	"	"	"	
12	"	"	"	"	"	
13	"	"	"	"	"	
14	"	"	"	"	"	
15	"	"	"	"	"	
16	"	"	"	"	"	B
17	"	"	"	"	"	

Notes: All passenger cars had doors (at each end of car) on same side.

A —Body of sweeper 9 at Topsail, Nfld., as of 1956.

B —Body of Birney 16 at Topsail, Nfld., as of 1956.

During unloading of cars in St. John's harbour in 1926, one Birney car slipped through its sling and landed on bottom of harbour—fortunately without any permanent ill effects!

Chateau Lake Louise and Alberta's snowy mountain peaks form a dramatic backdrop for car No. 51.

•21•
Lake Louise Tramway

THOSE WHO HAVE VISITED LAKE LOUISE, Alberta, in the Canadian Rockies, are aware of the fact that the Canadian Pacific Railway station is some four miles distant from the Lake proper, with its famed backdrop of the Victoria Glacier. The station is also some eight hundred feet lower in altitude.

After 1930, busses took hotel guests from the railway station to the Chateau Lake Louise and Deer Lodge, a much less interesting means of transportation as far as the rail enthusiast is concerned, since the station and hotel were once linked by a 42-inch gauge "tramway" operated by the Canadian Pacific Railway, but now out of existence for over seventy years. The road bed is still plainly to be seen, and forms an interesting hiking or bridle path for visitors to the Lake Louise resort area.

It was in 1912 that the railway, seeking more reliable and dependable means of transportation than horse-drawn vehicles hitherto used between the station and the chalet at the lake, envisioned and constructed the Lake Louise Tramway. As constructed, the tramway extended officially "from a point in Section 28, Township 28, Range 16, west of the 5th Meridian, to a point in Section 20, Township 28,

Range 16, west of the 5th Meridian". The line was opened in July 1912, and had a main-line length of 3.61 miles. It started on the opposite side of the railway station from the CPR main line, curved sharply in a semicircle, crossing the Bow River, and started its steep ascent of the foothills of the main range of the Rocky Mountains. The line, in plan, was in "switchback" fashion, with sharp curves at the angles. Its upper end was the CPR hotel at Lake Louise, where there was a carhouse and a loop, and a covered platform with covered passageway from platform to hotel. At the lower end of the line, Laggan (later Lake Louise station), the cars were turned originally on a turntable; later a loop was provided.

Original rolling stock on this line included two 28-foot open-bench "gasolene" passenger cars, each seating 35 and weighing about ten tons; also, two freight motors using the same design of frame as the passenger cars. All of this equipment was propelled by internal-combustion engines of the same type, a contemporary account states, as those "used in touring automobiles". Like the proverbial Toonerville trolley, the cars met all the trains at the station, including such famed favourites of the past as the Imperial

Car No. 50 at Canadian Pacific's Angus Shops, Montreal, where it was built in 1925. Note "Canadian Pacific" lettering, which was changed to "Lake Louise Tramway" upon arrival in Alberta.

Limited and the Trans-Canada Limited. The passenger cars were CPR Nos. 40 and 41, while the freight cars were 48 and 49. All were delivered on July 31st 1912. These cars were all of the 4-2-0 wheel arrangement.

After a year and a half of use, it was determined that a third passenger car could be more useful than a second freight motor, and accordingly, in April 1914, No. 48 was rebuilt into passenger car 42.

The line closed down in the winter season, its period of operation corresponding with the open season for the CPR hotel at Lake Louise, roughly May to September. The line possessed no snowplow equipment, so that winter operation could not have been undertaken. Repairs were made in the running shed at Lake Louise.

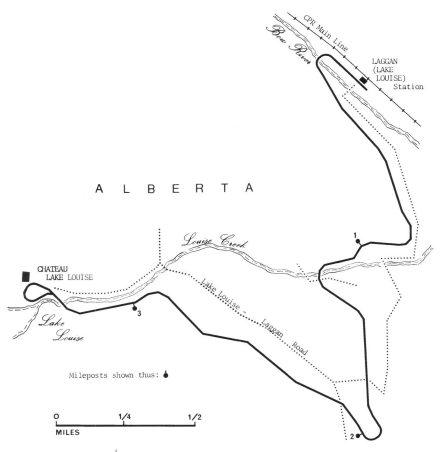

In 1925, the original equipment was supplemented by two additional passenger cars, closed vehicles this time, which much resembled street railway cars. Unlike the original open-bench cars, the new cars were double-trucked, and propelled by Sterling "Seabull" gasoline engines having six cylinders and 150 horsepower capacity. The fuel capacity was 34 Imperial gallons, and the cars seated 43, though it is recorded that car 51 was tested with a capacity load of 68 passengers and baggage. The cars weighed

OMER LAVALLÉE COLLECTION

Open bench car No. 40 embarking passengers at Canadian Pacific's Lake Louise Railway Station.

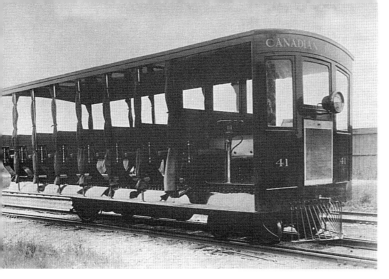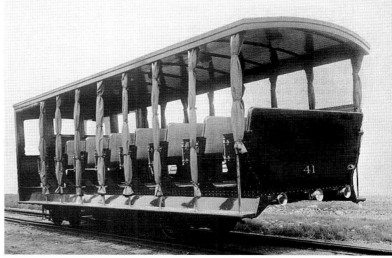

Open bench car No. 41 was really a "char-a-banc" bus chassis mounted on flanged wheels.

Baggage motor No. 49. A sister car, No. 48, was rebuilt into passenger car 42.

Another view of baggage motor No. 49, fitted with extended roof and removable seats for quick conversion to either baggage or passenger use.

Lake Louise passenger motor No. 40 and baggage trailer in World War I era, judging by the skirt lengths!

only 34,000 lbs. These two cars arrived at Lake Louise on May 27th 1925; they were lettered "Canadian Pacific" as was the other equipment but in the interim, while they were en route to the west, it was decided to reletter them to "Lake Louise Tramway", and accordingly, all equipment identification was changed.

The Lake Louise Tramway came under the jurisdiction of the Canadian Pacific Railway's Hotel Department. The frequency of operation was as high as thirty round-trips a day. The cars met all scheduled CPR transcontinental trains, as well as passenger extras. Operation of the line was carried out by a

telephone system linking the termini, but a form of train order terminal clearance was also used. There was a passing-track about halfway up the line, which the "up" tram always tried to make first in case the "down" tram's brakes didn't hold!

In the latter years, the 1912 equipment was kept as standby rolling stock for unusual crowds and tour groups. The remaining freight motor, No. 49, was adapted to passenger use with the provision of removable benches. Service on this line passed with the end of the 1930 season. The cars were removed from inventory in November 1930, and subsequently scrapped. The rails were taken up in 1931.

Lake Louise Tramway

Laggan* (CPR) to Chateau Lake Louise at Lake Louise, Alta. .... 3.61 miles aban.
* Now Lake Louise.

Gauge: 3 feet, 6 inches.

Chronology:

1912	—Canadian Pacific Railway Company builds Lake Louise Tramway for use during summer season only to take passengers and their baggage from transcontinental main line at Laggan (now Lake Louise) to the Canadian Pacific hotel Chateau Lake Louise.
1930	—Railway abandoned at close of hotel season.
1930, Nov	—All rolling stock removed from inventory.

Gasoline-mechanical railcars

No.	Builder	Year	C/N	Type	Weight	H.P.	From	To	Notes
40	CP Angus	1912	—	2-A	10 tons		New	x 1931	A
41	"	"	—	"	"		"	"	A
42	"	"	—	"	"		#48 4/14	"	B
48	"	"	—	"			New	#42 4/14	B
49	"	"	—	"			"	x1931	C
50	"	1925	—	2-B	17 tons	150	"	"	D
51	"	"	—	"	"	"	"	"	D

Notes: A—Cross-bench open-side cars much like open street cars of slightly earlier period.
       B—No. 48 was a motor flat car for baggage, rebuilt in April 1914 into a third passenger car like 40 and 41.
       C—No. 49 built as motor flat car for baggage and remained so.
       D—Nos. 50 and 51 were closed passenger cars.

•22•
Windsor Electric Street Railway Company

THE DISTINCTION OF HAVING OPERATED the first electric street railway in Canada belongs to the city of Windsor, Ontario, where such a line was inaugurated in June 1886. This predated electric railway systems in other cities of Canada by five or six years.

This pioneer application concerns our study because it was built to the 3'6" gauge, the same width adopted by four animal-powered street railways elsewhere in Ontario, and by the electric transit system which was constructed subsequently to serve St. John's, Newfoundland.

The Windsor Electric Street Railway Company was organized early in 1886 at the instance of Richard Bangham, a city councillor, who is said to have become a protagonist of electric railways through a visit in 1885 to the Exhibition in Toronto, where an experimental electric railway was a feature attraction in that year. Bangham had also revisited his native Brighton, England, at about the same time, and had returned to Canada vastly impressed by Volk's Electric Railway at that British seaside resort.

Bangham enlisted the aid of J. W. Tringham of Windsor, who passed for what would today be called an electrical engineer, and in the spring of 1886, they constructed a 1¼-mile main line between Windsor and its suburb of Walkerville, equipping it with a single electric motor car. The electrification was on the Van Depoele System, utilizing a 15-horsepower generator at the power plant. The current was collected from two overhead wires on which a little four-wheeled "troller" ran, connected to the motor car by flexible cables. As the car moved along, it pulled the troller with it; as the car came to a stop, the troller gradually overtook it and its own momentum carried it forward until the cables became taut and the troller was stopped. Occasionally, the motorman would stop fairly suddenly, the slack in the cable would run out

Canada's first commercial electric railway operation in Windsor, Ontario in 1886.

and stop the troller suddenly, derailing it and causing it to drop on the roof of the car with an alarming "thud". This characteristic of the Van Depoele system did not endear it to passengers who were apprehensive enough of the whole concept of moving cars by "the power of the lightning", and the troller soon gave way to under-running overhead collection with trolleys or pantographs, or third rail collection.

Public pride at the achievement of one of North America's earliest electric railways was reflected in an editorial in the Windsor *Record*, which afforded itself an opportunity to good-naturedly deride Windsor's larger and more affluent neighbour on the other side of the Detroit River.

"Windsor deserves to be the proud. Its citizens have a manifest right to tilt their heads at several degrees further back and to swell out their chests several inches forward. We have an electric street railway. No other place in Canada has such a road. Detroit has been dreaming about such an enterprise for some time, but the slow people of that place hadn't the nerve to tackle such a novel enterprise until they had seen how Windsor got along with it."

"The problem has been solved. The railway is a reality, as we can now scoot up to Walkerville on a streak of lightning, and we'll soon have the same motive power for our trip to Sandwich and beyond. Bully for Windsor! Hurrah for Tringham!"

Unfortunately for this pioneer electric railway, Tringham died later in the summer of 1886, and while the electric car ran until the autumn of that year, again in the summer of 1887 and perhaps in 1888 as well, the Company had taken out "insurance" in the form of eight horses and four Horsecars by the summer of 1888.

By that year also, the standard gauge horse railway of the Sandwich, Windsor & Amherstburg Railway Company had reached a length of 3¾ miles, and there was yet another animal-powered railway, the City Railway Company of Windsor, with a length of 4½ miles.

Faced with this competition, the electric railway that had reverted to a horsecar system was shortly thereafter discontinued and its operations absorbed.

•23•
Animal Powered Municipal Railways

A BRIEF ACCOUNT OF FOUR STREET RAILways in Ontario towns, using animal traction, concludes our analysis of Canadian common carrier narrow gauge railways.

These systems functioned in the cities of Kingston, Belleville, Brantford and St. Thomas. All were built uniformly to a gauge of 3'6" and in this choice, they may have been influenced by their proximity to Toronto which was the headquarters of the Toronto & Nipissing and Toronto, Grey & Bruce main line systems, which comprised the lion's share of Canadian small-width railways at this period.

Narrow gauge municipal railways were not without precedent on this continent, however, and a number of them could be found in the United States which were contemporary with the four Ontario lines.

Kingston

The Kingston Street Railway Company was incorporated on February 10th 1876, with a perpetual franchise and succeeded in establishing horsecar service within a year. The first horsecar appeared on Princess Street on February 2nd 1877, the car shed and stables being located at the rear of 493 Princess Street.

By 1889, the Company reported owning thirty horses and ten cars, operating over four miles of track laid with nine-pound rail (possibly metal straps on wooden timbers).

On May 27th 1893, the Kingston, Portsmouth & Cataraqui Street Railway Company was organized to take over the horsecar system and construct an electric street railway to standard gauge. The conversion of the narrow gauge railway began on July 2nd 1893, and initial electric operation by the successor company commenced on Princess Street late in September of the same year.

Kingston, Ontario horse car at King and Brock Streets in 1893. An extra team was used on Princess Street hill.

Belleville

While the date of incorporation of the Belleville Street Railway Company is unknown, it is said to have been opened in 1877. Its 2¼-mile route extended from the Grand Trunk Railway station to the government dock. The fare was six tickets for 25 cents. In 1889, the Company reported possessing five passenger cars, five other vehicles and twelve horses, and using 25-lb. rail.

A new company, the Belleville Traction Company, was formed in 1895 to take over the original company, to relay the track with heavier iron rails and electrify the operation on the Canadian General Electric System. It seems probable that the gauge was converted to standard at this stage.

By 1898, the Company was in financial difficulties because it reportedly did not serve the residential district, and after having been offered for sale in 1900 and again in 1901 with no bids being received, it was closed down in September 1901. Belleville thus achieved the dubious distinction of having been the first Canadian municipality to abandon a rail transit system.

Brantford

The Brantford Street Railway Company was incorporated in 1879 to build an animal-powered street railway in the city and township of Brantford. The date of opening of service is unknown.

It is reported as possessing 22 horses and seven cars in 1889, and operating over five miles of track laid with 30-lb. rail. In the course of the 1890s, the system was standard gauged and electrified, eventually forming part of the Grand Valley Railway Company, later becoming part of the Brantford Municipal Railway.

St. Thomas

The St. Thomas Street Railway Company was incorporated in 1878 to build an animal-powered street railway in that city and in adjoining municipalities. The date of inauguration of the system is not known, but it enjoyed a municipal franchise granted for fifty years. In 1889, the line possessed five cars, pulled by nine horses and operating over two miles of track laid with 30-lb. rail.

Early in 1896, the system was purchased by Colonel Stacey of St. Thomas and in 1898, an agreement was reached with the municipality to replace the narrow gauge horsecar line with an electric standard gauge operation. At this time, the length of line was the same as a decade earlier, but reported only four cars and eight horses.

The conversion seems to have been carried out in 1898 or 1899.

Mining and Tourist Railways on Canada's West Coast

About the Contributor

Eric Johnson was born in 1933 in Elk Point, Alberta, Canada. He spent ten years working in Alberta, Saskatchewan, British Columbia, and Yukon in construction, oilfields, and mines. A resident of Vancouver, British Columbia since 1964, he graduated from the University of British Columbia in 1966 with a BSc in chemistry. For twenty-eight years, he was a forest products research laboratory technologist.

Eric is a member of the Canadian Railroad Historical Association's Pacific Coast Division, and of the Pacific Great Eastern/British Columbia Railways Special Interest Group. Author of: *Mining Railways of the Klondike* (1995); *The Bonanza Narrow Gauge Railway—the Story of the Klondike Mines Railway* (1997); *The Sea-to-Sky Gold Rush Route—A Guide to the Scenic Railway of the White Pass and Yukon Route* (1998).

Part 1:

Wellington Colliery Railway narrow gauge lines

The narrow gauge coal mining railways of Vancouver Island have never been described in adequate detail and no complete roster of equipment has ever been published. The railway is so well known and was so long-lived, yet much data is maddeningly unknown, and what is available is often conflicting. The description that follows is thus necessarily vague. Sources have been noted below.

Coal deposits inland from the coastal settlement of Nanaimo, British Columbia, had been known by Aboriginals many years before the coming of Europeans, but not until 1869 were the deposits exploited commercially. That year Dunsmuir, Diggle and Company began mining the deposits at what had become the Wellington Colliery. First shipments to Departure Bay, north of Nanaimo, were made with horses or mules and wagon over roads, and later over an inclined steel-shod, wooden-railed, cable-operated tramway of 30-inch gauge. By 1874, cars were hauled by traction engines modified to work on rails. In 1878, part-owner Robert Dunsmuir bought the company's first "real" locomotive, a 30-inch gauge 0-6-0T (Baldwin c/n 3940), which was named the *Duke of Wellington*. Soon thereafter a second almost identical machine (Baldwin c/n 4424) arrived, named the *Duchess of Wellington*—one worked chiefly from the mine, the other at the Departure Bay docks. The railway had been rerouted and comprised about ten miles of track. In 1883, Dunsmuir bought out his partner, Diggle, and he officially chartered the railway as the Wellington Colliery Railway.

In the meanwhile a new company, the East Wellington Colliery, opened a mine nearby and built a 36-inch gauge railway leading to Departure Bay. Power there was provided by two saddle-tank locomotives named the *Premier* (c/n 4356, an 0-6-0T

Believed to be the Duke of Wellington, *this 30-inch gauge Baldwin 0-6-0T locomotive, c/n 3940, was the first to arrive at Robert Dunsmuir's Wellington Colliery. Dunsmuir himself (in the stovepipe hat), and his wife, pose beside the locomotive above Departure Bay, Nanaimo, British Columbia. A similar locomotive, Baldwin c/n 4424, the* Duchess of Wellington, *arrived soon thereafter.*

built by Baldwin, Burnham, Parry & Williams in 1878) and the *Columbia*. Seven years later, Dunsmuir acquired the East Wellington Colliery and its railway, which he combined with his Wellington Colliery Railway. Dunsmuir's 30-inch gauge Baldwins, and the railway, were probably rebuilt to 36-inch at that time. Later, Dunsmuir also built standard gauge lines from other coal properties to connect with the mainline Esquimalt and Nanaimo Railway. As late as 1898, the narrow gauge lines were still in use, with six locomotives in operation, but the remaining narrow gauge lines and some of the locomotives were standard gauged in the early 1900s.

In Nanaimo today, only one of the narrow gauge locomotives remains, on display: Baldwin c/n 9869, a 0-6-0T engine of 36-inch gauge, built in March 1889 and lettered as the *Wellington*, but said by some to

actually be the *Victoria*. It had been standard gauged, but was regauged to the original for display. The other remaining locomotive is the *Duchess* (originally the *Duchess of Wellington*), used on the White Pass and Yukon Route's 36-inch gauge Taku Tram only from 1900 until 1919, and later moved to its present location at Carcross, Yukon.

A three-and-one-half mile narrow gauge railway utilizing one saddle-tank locomotive was operated for short time in the late 1800s at the Baynes Sound Colliery near Comox, British Columbia. No adequate description of this property has been found to exist.

Sources: data provided by the British Columbia Provincial Archives; *The History of a Railway*, Robert Swanson, 1960; and *Vancouver Island Railroads*, Robert Turner, 1973, reissued 1997.

Late in its life—probably in 1903—on the NAT&TCo's Cliff Creek railway, Porter locomotive c/n 1972 pauses before leaving mines, 1½ miles upgrade from the Yukon River loadout, with six of its coal wagons.

The date is August 3rd 1903, and on the foredeck of the steamboat Mary Graff *at Dawson City, Yukon, are two well-used locomotives. On the left is Porter c/n 1167, on the right Porter c/n 922. They are bound for the Coal Creek railway, located 54 miles downstream on a waterway that feeds the Yukon River.*

Part 2: Narrow Gauge Mining Railways of the Klondike

Three short-lived, long-forgotten, 36-inch gauge railways operated in the Yukon between 1899 and 1915, two as coal haulers, the other hauling gold-bearing ground for sluicing. The railways were not chartered common carriers, but industrial railways built to serve only the owners' businesses. It is interesting to note that, of the eight locomotives used on these three railways, six still exist—certainly one of the highest proportion of locomotive preservation known.

Contrary to some beliefs, the great Klondike gold discovery of 1896 did not just "happen" overnight. For twenty years prior, prospectors had been working the great Yukon River for placer gold, and by 1886 a significant strike was made up the Fortymile River, Yukon, a feeder of the Yukon River. At the river's mouth, fifty miles downstream from what would later become Dawson City, the substantial town of Fortymile grew. Prospectors worked every stream in the area, and soon discovered low grade lignite (coal) deposits on Cliff Creek, eight miles downriver from Fortymile, and on Coal Creek, whose mouth is four miles downriver from Fortymile.

Not until the great Klondike Gold Rush of 1897 did the coal discoveries become of commercial interest. With the booming of Dawson City at the mouth of the Klondike River, heating fuel became a critical resource in a land where overnight temperatures dropped below freezing for eight or more months each year. Wood, which became the principal fuel, immediately led to the development of a huge industry—but coal gradually made inroads.

In 1899 the North American Transportation and Trading Company (NAT&TCo), its Yukon trading post and office based at Fortymile, began construction of a railway, as well as mining and shipping camps, on Cliff Creek. The grade of the 1½-mile railway, from the Yukon River up to the mines, was a steep 5% or greater grade. In July that year a brand-new 0-4-0T locomotive and more than a dozen wood-bodied coal wagons arrived and went to work. Mining carried on for most of the following seasons, and coal was stockpiled, since shipping to Dawson was done by steamboats on the Yukon River only between the months of May (ice breakup) and October (freeze up). The Cliff Creek mine was worked out by mid-summer of 1903, although riverside stockpiles lasted into 1904. However, in August 1903, the NAT&TCo's Porter locomotive was sold and shipped to the Coal Creek Coal Company (CCCCo), which was just beginning construction of its railway only four miles upstream on the Yukon River. Track was salvaged from the Cliff Creek railway in 1918.

The CCCCo began construction of its 12-mile railway early in the summer of 1903. The line had a relatively flat grade of average less than 1%. First on the scene was the ex-NAT&TCo 0-4-0T locomotive in early August, soon followed by delivery of two larger 0-6-0T locomotives, both of which were second-hand and rebuilt. Along with them came some rebuilt flat cars. Mining and shipping activities commenced that year. By June 1905, the CCCCo sold the ex-NAT&TCo locomotive to the newly-chartered Tanana Mines Railroad, soon renamed the Tanana Valley Railroad (TVR), of Fairbanks, Alaska. The TVR was absorbed by the Alaska Railroad in 1917, which utilized the little Porter until 1930 when it was put on display in Fairbanks. More than sixty years later, a band of rail enthusiasts acquired and restored the locomotive which today operates seasonally on a short tourist line in that city.

In 1906, the CCCCo operation on Coal Creek was taken over by the Sourdough Coal Company (SCCo) which held coal lands adjacent to the original CCCCo property. The new company operated the mine and railway until early 1909 when it and other Dawson properties were acquired by a new company financed in England, the Northern Light, Power and Coal Company (NLP&CCo). The NLP&CCo bought a new two-truck Lima Shay and additional rolling stock. It announced grandiose plans for a coal-fired electrical power plant at the Coal Creek mine site, with a 40-mile transmission line to Dawson. Coal was shipped to Dawson, but not until the next year did shipments of the power-generating machinery begin arriving at Coal Creek for setup. The transmission lines were eventually completed, but less than one-half of the generating plant was made operational. The perceived market for electricity did not develop, and the power plant was operated only periodically, finally being shut down by the NLP&CCo in 1912, although mining and shipping of coal to Dawson continued.

In early 1913, the Canadian Klondyke (sic) Mining Company (CKMCo)—which operated electrically-powered dredges along the Klondike River near Dawson—leased the complete NLP&CCo plant at Coal Creek. However, in the meantime, the NLP&CCo had sold the Lima Shay to a gold mine at Juneau, Alaska. It was scrapped in Washington State in 1940. Left at Coal Creek were the two worn-out 0-6-0T Porters. Two of the CKMCo's little-used 0-4-0T Porters (brought to Dawson in 1904) were taken to Coal Creek. They worked there until 1914, when the CKMCo's lease was terminated by court action. It is believed coal was shipped from the Coal

Creek mine into 1915. In 1918, the generating plant and rail were salvaged, but the four locomotives and some rolling stock were abandoned at the mouth of Coal Creek. One of the locomotives was lost in the Yukon River; the other three still exist today, retrieved by private individuals in 1969.

Back in 1903, at the mouth of Bear Creek on the Klondike River four miles east of Dawson, the CKMCo had its placer gold operation underway. The mining was done manually. In 1904, the company brought in four new Porter 0-4-0T locomotives, two Marion steam shovels, twenty steel-bodied dump cars, and rails. Not a very efficient operation, the shovels scooped loads of gold-bearing gravel into the cars. These were then hauled over constantly-repositioned tracks to a sluicing plant on the Klondike River. An ill-conceived plant, it was replaced the next year by a dredge. The locomotives then saw only sporadic action on the rails of Klondike Mines Railway in Dawson, at a new dredge construction site, and until the tracks were lifted in 1913. Thereafter, the two remaining locomotives sat unused at the Bear Creek camp until the 1960s, when the then-owner, the Yukon Consolidated Gold Corporation, sold one to a private owner, and donated the other to the Dawson City Museum. Both Porters survive today. The site of the railway on Bear Creek was later thoroughly worked over by dredges, and no trace of the lines can be found today.

YUKON ARCHIVES; DAWSON CITY MUSEUM COLLECTION, PRINT NO. 6337

In the summer of 1903, Coal Creek locomotive, Porter c/n 922, is at work finishing up the rail grade, 12 miles in length from the Yukon River to the coal mines at the head of the creek.

ROSTER:
Locomotives of the three 36-inch gauge mining railways of the Klondike—from the oldest to youngest

Porter c/n 922: 0-6-0T weighing about 12-tons. Built April 1888 by H.K. Porter of Pittsburgh, PA for Spokane and Montrose Motor Railroad (S&MMR), Spokane, WA. Assignment/location 1892 to 1902 unknown. 1903: locomotive purchased by Coal Creek Coal Company (CCCCo) for its railway at Coal Creek, Yukon. No known road number. 1906: CCCCo taken over by the Sourdough Coal Company (SCCo). 1909: SCCo taken over by Northern Light, Power and Coal Company (NLP&CCo). June 1918: locomotive abandoned at Coal Creek. March 1969: recovered by Gunnar Nilsson of Whitehorse, Yukon. 1993: donated to present owner, Yukon Transportation Museum in Whitehorse. Status: cosmetically-restored.

Porter c/n 1167: 0-6-0T weighing about 14-tons. Built April 1890 for S&MMR. Assignment/location 1892 to 1902 unknown. 1903: locomotive purchased by CCCCo. No known road number. 1906: CCCCo taken over by SCCo. 1909: SCCo taken over by NLP&CCo. June 1918: locomotive abandoned at Coal Creek. March 1969: recovered by Harry Copper of Whitehorse, Yukon. 1992: sold to present owner Dick Gilbert of Jake's Corner, Yukon. Status: located south of Whitehorse, Yukon, unrestored.

Porter c/n 1972: 0-4-0T weighing 7 tons. Built March 1899 for railway of North American Transportation and Trading Company (NAT&TCo) located at Cliff Creek, Yukon. No road number known. July 1903: locomotive sold to CCCCo. June 1905: sold to the Tanana Valley Railroad (TVR), Fairbanks, AK. 1919: TVR taken over by Alaska Railroad, Fairbanks, AK. From 1930 until early 1990s, locomotive on static display in Fairbanks. Subsequently acquired by a railfan group, Friends of Tanana Valley Railroad Inc., which restored locomotive. Status: running summer-only, on short section of track in Fairbanks.

Porter c/n 3022: 0-4-0T weighing 7 tons. Built April 1904 for Detroit Yukon Mining Company (DYMCo), Dawson City, Yukon, with road No. 1. June 1905: DYMCo absorbed by Canadian Klondyke (sic) Mine Company (CKMCo), Dawson City, Yukon. 1921: CKMCo absorbed by Burrall and Baird (B&B). 1925: B&B absorbed by Yukon Consolidated Gold Corporation (YCGC). 1965: locomotive sold to Roger Brammall of Vancouver Island. Status: located at Shawnigan Lake, British Columbia, unrestored.

Porter c/n 3023: 0-4-0T weighing 7 tons. Built April 1904 for DYMCo, with road No. 2. June 1905: DYMCo absorbed by CKMCo. 1913: CKMCo leased CCCCo property; shipped locomotive to Coal Creek, where abandoned 1918. Locomotive reportedly was parked on trestle high above Yukon River, and plunged into river when trestle collapsed in late 1930s.

Porter c/n 3024: 0-4-0T weighing 7 tons. Built April 1904 for DYMCo, with road no. 3. June 1905: DYMCo absorbed by CKMCo. 1913: operators of CKMCo leased CCCCo property; shipped locomotive to Coal Creek, where abandoned June 1918. March 1969: recovered by Dan Nowlan of Whitehorse, Yukon. 1983: sold to present owner Keith Christenson of Eagle River, AK. Status: unrestored at Eagle River, AK.

Porter c/n 3025: 0-4-0T weighing 7 tons. Built April 1904 for DYMCo, with road no. 4. June 1905: DYMCo absorbed by CKMCo. 1921: CKMCo absorbed by B&B. 1925: B&B absorbed by YCGC. May 1961: YCGC donated locomotive to Dawson City Museum, Dawson, Yukon. Status: on display, cosmetically-restored.

Lima Shay c/n 2190 weighing 24 tons: Built July 1909 by Lima Locomotive Works, Lima, OH for NLP&CCo. No known road number. June 1913: sold to Alaska Gastineau Mining Company (AGMCo) of Juneau, AK. No known road number. March 1921: locomotive sold to Puget Sound Machinery Depot (PSMD), Seattle, WA, road no. 2. 1921: sold to Biles-Coleman Lumber Company of Omak, WA. Later relettered as no. 102. Scrapped 1940 at Omak.

In the summer of 1904, a newly-acquired Marion steam shovel and one (believed to be locomotive No. 1) of four new Porter locomotives are in the process of moving gold-bearing gravel to a washing plant not far away. That would be the only summer the DYMCo locomotives would work at their intended use.

At Bear Creek near Dawson City, one of DYMCo's Marion steam shovels, rigged out as a crane, is unloading parts for a dredge. Probably taken in early 1905, DYMCo locomotive No. 1 is shoving the chassis of a mine car, now fitted up as a flat car. The more-efficient dredging process will soon replace the shovels, locomotives and track that required constant repositioning.

ERIC JOHNSON

Built by Lisbon Portugal Tramways in 1925, where it operated until 1978, the Whitehorse Waterfront Trolley *is a 24-passenger summer-only tourist attraction, running back-and-forth (no turns) on former WP&YR trackage. It tows its own 600-volt generator mounted on a trailer.*

The Whitehorse *Waterfront Trolley*

In 2000, the Miles Canyon Historical Railway Society (MCHRS), in Whitehorse, began operating car No. 531, a 36-inch gauge two-axle tram, on a 1½ kilometre section of WP&YR track along the Yukon River within Whitehorse city limits. Another 1 kilometre of track was scheduled for use in 2005. Running forward and backward, with no loops or wyes, the trolley is a summer-only tourist attraction. The tram was built in 1925 by the Santa Amaro of Lisbon Portugal Tramways, where it was operated until 1978. Purchased then by the Lake Superior Railroad Museum (Minnesota), it was resold in 1999 to the Yukon Territorial Government which had it restored and rewired in Seattle. The MCHRS manages and operates the trolley, a ten-ton car with seating for twenty-four. No. 531 originally drew power in Portugal from a catenary line, but now tows its own 600-volt generator mounted on a small speeder trailer. The trolley is housed in the old, relocated WP&YR engine house, saved from demolition by the MCHRS and other agencies.

Copper Belt Railway

Owned and operated by the MCHRS since 1998, the Copper Belt Railway is located near McIntyre Creek at mile 919 on the Alaska Highway (north of Whitehorse). A summer-only operation, the line presently has 1.8 kilometres of 24-inch gauge track laid in the shape of an elongated figure eight. Motive power comprises two used one-cylinder diesel-engined mining locomotives of ten and twenty horsepower that were refurbished by students of Yukon College. The Copper Belt Railway has a twenty-passenger coach, open sided but roofed, and a maintenance-of-way flat car. On the ten-acre site is a picnic ground, an abandoned mining adit, and a large station built from a 1906 design. The station also serves as a museum.

Below: Business Car No. 1 "Terra Nova" was between assignments at St. John's when photographed on June 20th 1956. This car has been preserved at the Canada Science & Techhnology Museum, Ottawa.